DEAR READERS & VIEWERS

The greeting is right, you are not mistaken. Finally, you can be readers and viewers at the same time, turning the pages of a single book! Yo

ding a simple book with fascinat ut this particular book is MUCH

WHAT MAKES THIS HYBRI

This hybrid media publication covers a wide range of interesting topics packed with animated shorts! Each chapter is full of cutting-edge technology: the reader does nothing but starts the animation on a mobile phone or tablet to become the viewer.

SNEAK PEEK...

What do we need to know about our cosmic home? What is inside the Earth? How does a volcano work? Why does the wind blow? How do rain clouds form? Numerous fascinating questions about the wonderful world around us, with spectacular animations.

A GUIDE FOR USING THE AR CONTENT

1. Download the **AR Books LibrARy** app.

arbooksliblibrary.com/app

2. Register and log in.

3. Follow the instructions in the app.

4. Book ID:

NATURESTUDY

We wish you an enjoyable reading & cinema experience!

The authors and the developers

1

OUR COSMIC HOME

Earth, which is the third planet in the Solar System, is the only celestial body in the universe known for sure to be inhabited. It is located at an ideal distance from the Sun to actively support life.

WHERE DO WE LIVE?

Our Solar System has eight "official" planets orbiting the Sun. Here they are listed in order of their distance from the Sun: Mercury, Venus, Earth, Mars, Jupiter, Saturn, Uranus, and Neptune. Our Earth is a **rocky/terrestrial planet**: it consists mainly of heavy elements and rock-forming minerals. Its shape is a slightly flattened sphere: its equatorial radius is larger than at the poles because of the rotation around its axis. Space images show that our planet appears bluish from space. This is because 71% of its surface is covered by water.

"MNEMONIC: MY VERY EDUCATED MOTHER JUST SERVED US NACHOS".

ETERNAL CIRCLE

The Earth **orbits** the Sun at an average distance of 150 million km in a roughly circular orbit once every 365 days and **rotates** about its axis once every 24 hours.

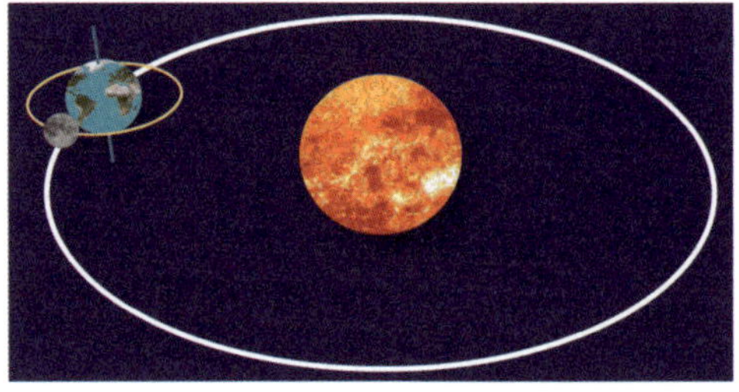

EARTH'S CLIMATE

The Sun's rays reach the Earth's surface at a decreasing angle as they move from the equator towards the poles, therefore, the **heating decreases** towards the poles. At a given point on the earth, the rays reach the surface at **different angles** at different times of the year causing seasonal differences in temperatures.

THE MYSTICAL MOON

The Moon is in a fixed orbit around the Earth. It plays an important role in stabilising the climate and shaping the tidal dynamics of water.

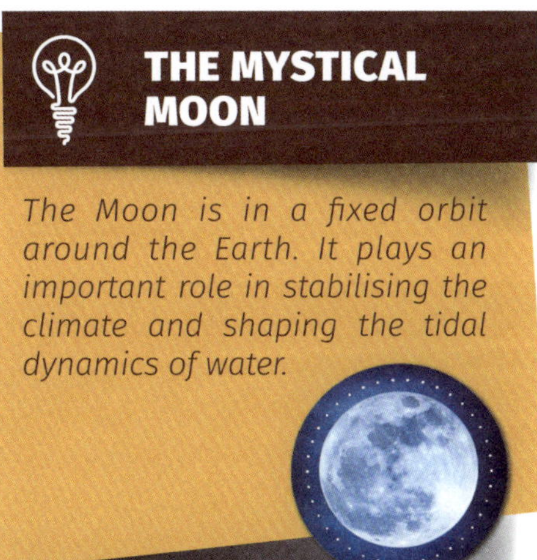

TEST YOUR KNOWLEDGE

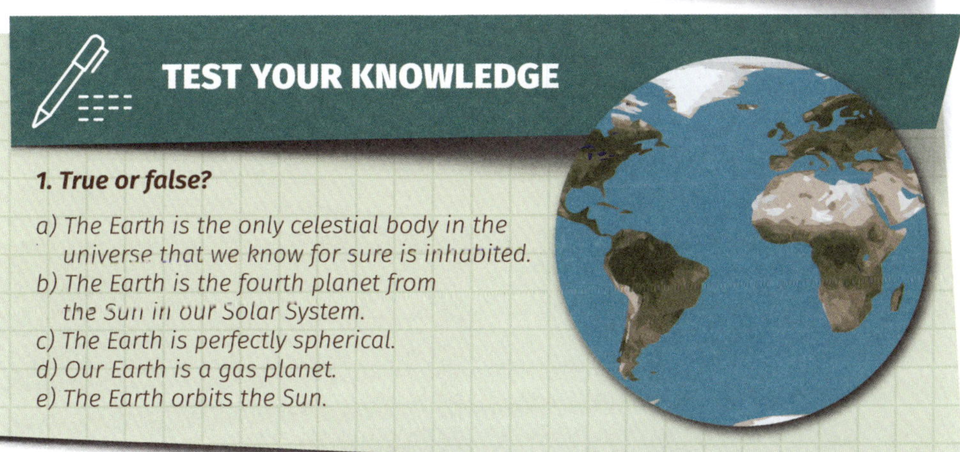

1. True or false?

a) The Earth is the only celestial body in the universe that we know for sure is inhabited.
b) The Earth is the fourth planet from the Sun in our Solar System.
c) The Earth is perfectly spherical.
d) Our Earth is a gas planet.
e) The Earth orbits the Sun.

2

OUR ETERNAL COMPANION

Our Earth has only one moon. We call it "the Moon" because for a long time it was the only one we knew about. The two celestial bodies form a gravitationally bound binary system in which two bodies orbit around a common centre of mass.

THE BIRTH OF THE MOON

The theory accepted today is that the planet Theia collided with the Earth during the formation of the Solar System about 4.5 billion years ago. The material, ejected by the **cosmic catastrophe**, formed the moon through gravitational accretion.

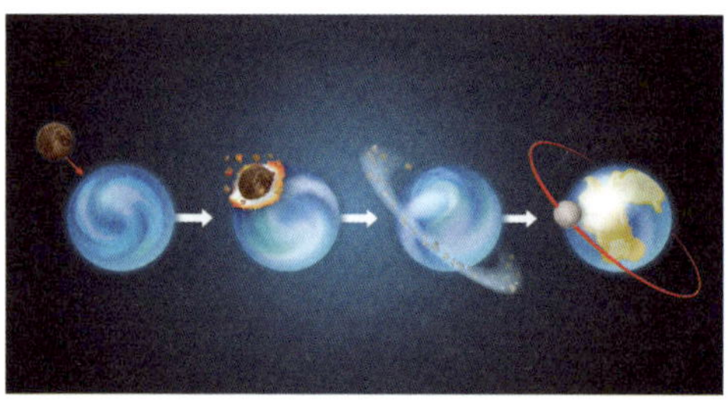

INTERESTING FACTS

- *In total, US astronauts have brought almost 400 kg of moon rocks back to Earth.*
- *The Moon is moving further and further away from our planet.*
- *The same side of the Moon is always facing the Earth.*

SOLAR ECLIPSE, LUNAR ECLIPSE

Sometimes the Moon, Earth, and Sun can line up exactly. If the Earth blocks the Moon from the Sun, it is a **lunar eclipse**, if the Moon blocks the Sun, it is a **solar eclipse**.

A STRANGE COINCIDENCE...

Seen from Earth, the Moon and the Sun appear to be almost exactly the same size, so that during a **total solar eclipse** the Moon completely covers the Sun's disc for a few minutes.

THE TIDAL PHENOMENON

Tides are very long-period waves that move through the oceans and seas in response to the forces exerted by the Moon and the Sun. The gravitational pull of the Moon and the Sun, the orbit of the Earth around the Sun, and the orbit of the Moon around the Earth form **tidal belts** in surface waters. The surface of the oceans and seas **periodically** rises and falls twice a day.

TEST YOUR KNOWLEDGE

1. Match the terms with the descriptions.
lunar eclipse, solar eclipse, Theia, moon rocks, total solar eclipse

a) US astronauts have brought almost 400 kilograms of them back to Earth.
b) The phenomenon of the Earth blocking the Moon from the Sun.
c) The phenomenon of the Moon blocking out the Sun from Earth's view.
d) 4.5 million years ago, during the formation of the Solar System, it collided with Earth.
e) The phenomenon in which the Moon completely covers the Sun's disk for a few minutes.

2. True or false?

a) US astronauts have brought a total of almost 400 kg of moon rocks back to Earth.
b) The Moon is moving closer and closer to our planet.
c) The Moon always turns the same side towards the Earth.

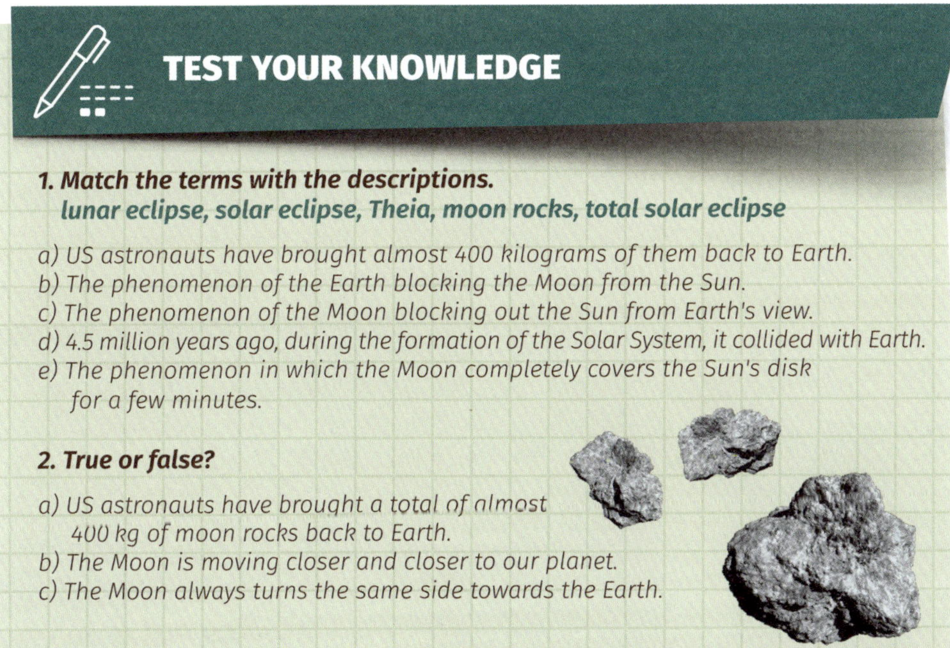

3 COLD & HOT

Like the Sun, the Earth has a spherical structure. Gravitational forces, cooling and the Earth's rotation have caused materials to separate according to their density and form spherical shells.

STRUCTURE OF THE EARTH

The Earth's spherical shells are called **geospheres.** The **inner spherical shells** are the Earth's core, mantle and crust. The **outer spherical shells** include the soil (pedosphere), the water (hydrosphere), the atmosphere, and the biosphere.

EARTH'S CRUSTS

Earth's crust is divided into two types: continental crust and oceanic crust. The upper layer of the **continental crust** is rich in silicates but poor in metals. The dominant rock is granite. Below this is the basaltic-gabbroic crust, which is rich in metals but poor in silicates. The simpler **oceanic crust** has the same structure under all the Earth's oceans. The upper layer is fine-grained basaltic, while the lower layer is coarser-grained gabbroic.

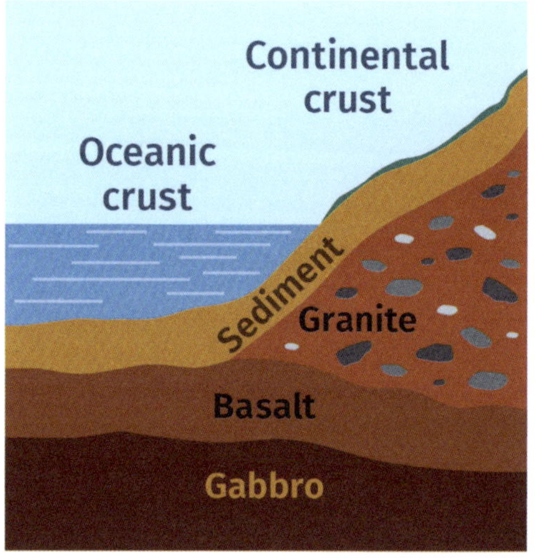

EARTH'S MANTLE

Below the Earth's crust lies the **mantle**. Towards the bottom, the proportion of silicates gradually decreases, and the proportion of heavier, metallic compounds increases. The upper, solid layer of the Earth's mantle and the crust above it together form the **shell** (lithosphere). The other layer of the Earth's mantle is the formless, soft mantle (asthenosphere), which consists of hot, glowing, flowing magma.

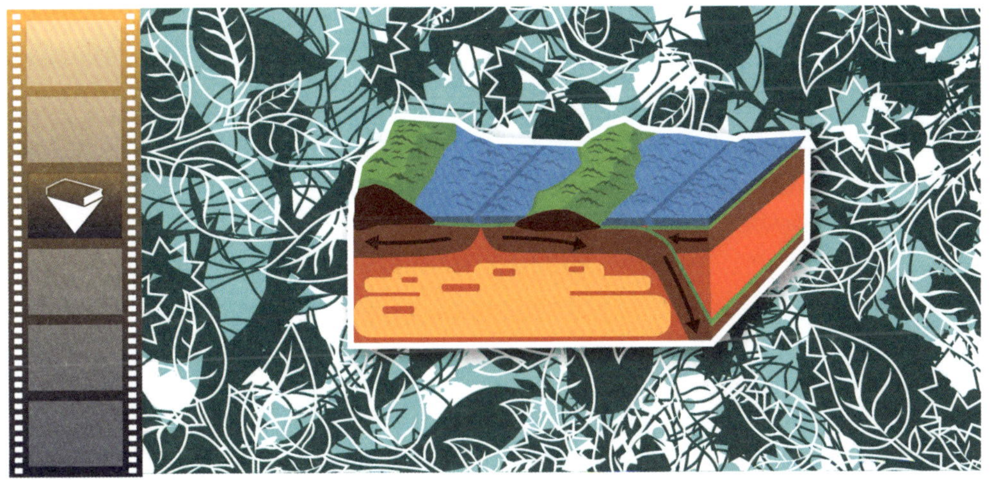

EARTH'S CORE

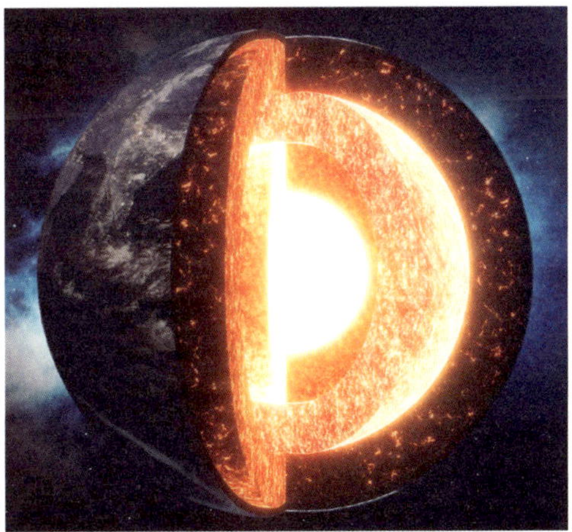

Earth's core is the very hot, very dense centre of our planet. The two parts of the Earth's core are the outer core and the inner core. In the liquid **outer core** (core-shell) there are turbulent flows of matter that generate electromagnetic fields. The **inner core** is solid because its components (iron, nickel, cobalt) do not melt at 5-6000 °C in the inner core due to the enormous pressure.

TEST YOUR KNOWLEDGE

1. True or false?

a) The Earth has a spherical structure, similar to the Sun.
b) The pedosphere is the soil mantle of the Earth.
c) The Earth's mantle is the outermost, solid spherical shell of our planet.
d) The crust is thicker under continents and thinner under the oceans.
e) The Earth's core consists of liquid metals, mainly nickel and gold.

4

BIRTH OF GIANTS

Mountains can form through folding, faulting, and volcanism. Fold mountains can be formed by the collision of two tectonic plates. Their surface is characterised by jagged, parallel ridges, steep slopes, and longitudinal valleys.

COLLISION OF PLATES

When **two oceanic plates** collide, the weaker one bends and the stronger one pushes underneath, lifting the edge of the upper one. Part of the underlying rock plate breaks up along the edge due to rock melting, and folds at the surface. Examples include the Japanese Islands, New Britain (Papua New Guinea), and the New Hebrides Archipelago (Melanesia). Deep-sea trenches run in the foreground of the **archipelagos**. When **oceanic and continental plates** collide, the thinner, denser oceanic plate pushes under the continental plate, creating a deep-sea trench. This is how the Andes of South America and the Cordilleras of North America were formed, for example. When **two continental plates** approach and then collide, initially an **ocean basin** is formed, and the thick ocean sediment subsequently folds. This is how the Himalayas and Mount Everest, the highest peak on Earth, were formed.

SUBDUCTION ZONE

When two oceanic plates collide or an oceanic plate collides with a continental plate, **deep-sea trenches** form in the subduction zone. Some of the accumulated ocean sediment melts as it enters the asthenosphere and erupts in violent volcanic explosions.

FAULT-BLOCKS MOUNTAINS

Fault-block mountains (or just **"block mountains"**) are formed by internal stress along fault lines or cracks in the crust. The pressure displaces large crustal blocks, forcing one side upwards and the other downwards.

TEST YOUR KNOWLEDGE

1. Match the process with the description.
collision of two oceanic plates / continental plates.

a) The mountain-building process begins with the formation of an ocean basin.
b) This is how volcanic rocks form archipelagos.

2. Match the natural formations with the way they were formed.
the Andes, the Japanese Islands, New Britain Archipelago, Cordillera, the Himalayas

a) When two oceanic plates collide.
b) Oceanic and continental plates collide.
c) When two continental plates collide.

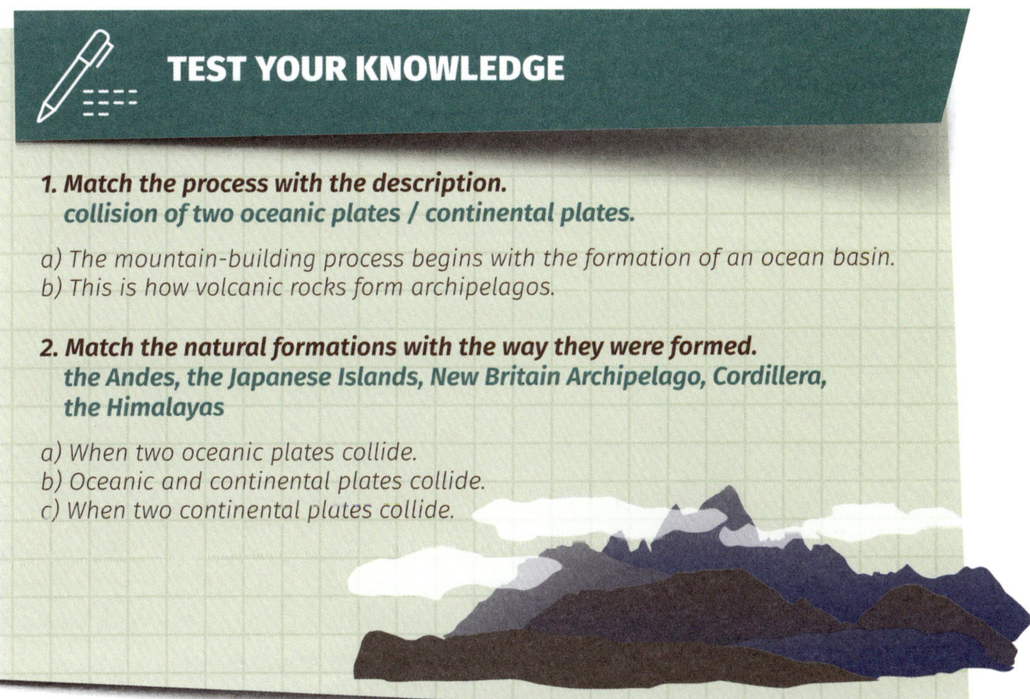

5

GIANTS ON FIRE

Volcanism is when glowing, malleable silicate – called magma – melts then erupts from the depths of the Earth. The magma that comes to the surface is called lava. Volcanic rocks are formed in the process.

FORMATION OF VOLCANOES

Volcanoes form at the **boundaries between tectonic plates**, typically near the coast. Europe's famous coastal volcanoes include Vesuvius, Mount Etna, and Stromboli (one of the most active volcanoes on Earth). Mid-ocean ridges form along receding plate margins. Deep trenches form at the junction of nearby plate margins. Material from the subducting plate sinks into the deep-sea trench and melts. This lava is denser, flows more slowly, and forms steeper volcanic cones. Their eruptions are accompanied with violent explosions.

VOLCANOES IN THE INNER AREAS OF TECTONIC PLATES

Volcanoes found in the middle of a tectonic plate are arranged **in a chain**. This is because an active volcano has a hot spot below it. The **hot spot** is the hole that the flowing magma has burned into the crust, allowing volcanic activity to occur. Over the course of a few hundred thousand years, the plate continues to move, and the hot spot burns a new hole in the crust. This is the case, for example, with the volcanic series of the Hawaiian Islands.

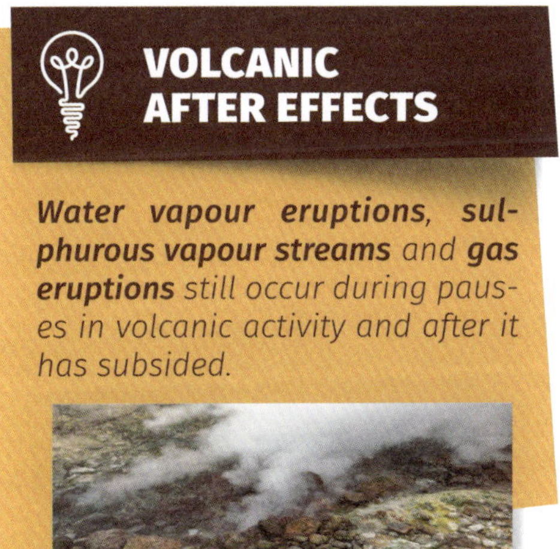

VOLCANIC AFTER EFFECTS

***Water vapour eruptions**, **sulphurous vapour streams** and **gas eruptions** still occur during pauses in volcanic activity and after it has subsided.*

VOLCANOES UNDER WATER

Pillow lava is a characteristic rock formation from submarine eruptions where hot extruding lava chills against cool sea water and rapidly forms a solid crust. Low viscosity basalt lava results in gently sloping shield volcanoes and flat basalt plateaus.

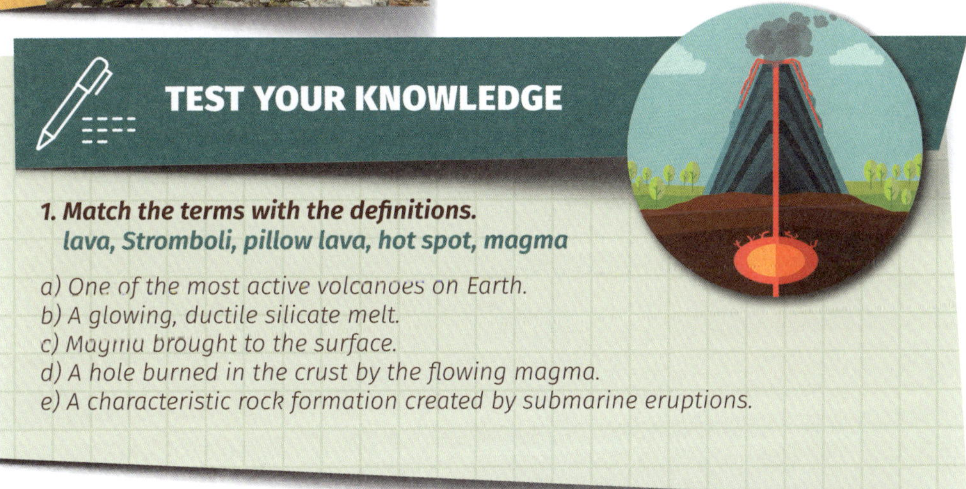

TEST YOUR KNOWLEDGE

1. Match the terms with the definitions.
lava, Stromboli, pillow lava, hot spot, magma

a) One of the most active volcanoes on Earth.
b) A glowing, ductile silicate melt.
c) Magma brought to the surface.
d) A hole burned in the crust by the flowing magma.
e) A characteristic rock formation created by submarine eruptions.

6 IT'S MOVING THERE!

Earthquakes are sudden shockwaves caused by the movement of tectonic plates at plate boundaries. Quake waves are triggered by pent-up internal stresses.

CAN EARTHQUAKES BE PREDICTED?

The movement of tectonic plates **away from** each other, **towards** each other, **or past each other** is called structural movement and results in **seismicity**, **folding**, **earthquakes**, and **volcanism**. Earthquakes release the stresses in solid rock masses resulting from plate movements. They are thus primarily the result of rock plate movements, but can also be triggered by volcanic eruptions or human activities (anthropogenic effects).

INTERESTING FACTS

Today, we still lack instruments that could accurately predict earthquakes. However, major disasters can be prevented by detecting small vibrations. The strange behaviours of some animals can also be used to predict danger. (Most scientists, however, do not support this idea.)

THE LARGEST EARTHQUAKES

The most powerful earthquake ever recorded was in Chile in **1960** with a **magnitude of 9.5**. Several severe earthquakes with many fatalities have been recorded in San Francisco, among other places. 80% of earthquakes occur at the edge of the Pacific basin and 15% in the area between the Mediterranean Sea and the Indonesian archipelago.

MEASURING EARTHQUAKES

A **seismograph** is an instrument used to measure the magnitude of an earthquake. An average of 700 000–800 000 earthquakes are recorded per year, of which about 300-400 have a high magnitude. **The Richter scale indicates the strength of an earthquake.** The scale has no upper limit, but values above 10 are practically unknown. The Mercalli scale expresses the extent of the damage caused by an earthquake.

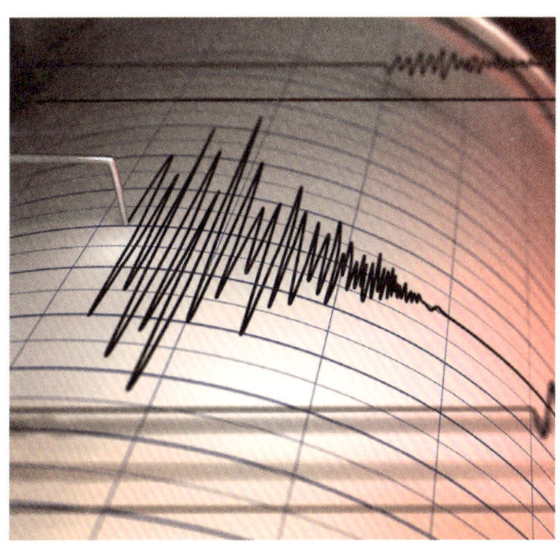

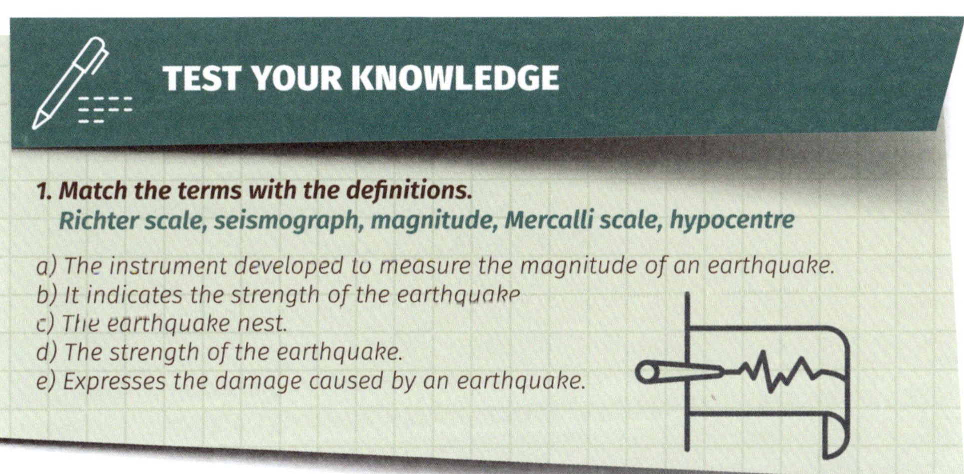

TEST YOUR KNOWLEDGE

1. Match the terms with the definitions.
Richter scale, seismograph, magnitude, Mercalli scale, hypocentre

a) The instrument developed to measure the magnitude of an earthquake.
b) It indicates the strength of the earthquake
c) The earthquake nest.
d) The strength of the earthquake.
e) Expresses the damage caused by an earthquake.

7 WONDERFUL STALACTITES

Most karst phenomena occur in limestone mountains. Karst phenomena refer to the processes of dissolution and the topographies that are formed during dissolution.

KARST PHENOMENA

Karst phenomena can be caused by dissolution and precipitation. They occur as a result of **water and CO_2 (weak carbonic acid) seeping through cracks** in the rock. The amount of carbon dioxide and thus the extent of dissolution varies with the thickness of the soil cover and the biological activity of the soil. A warm, humid climate typically produces more karstification due to thick topsoil and abundant biota.

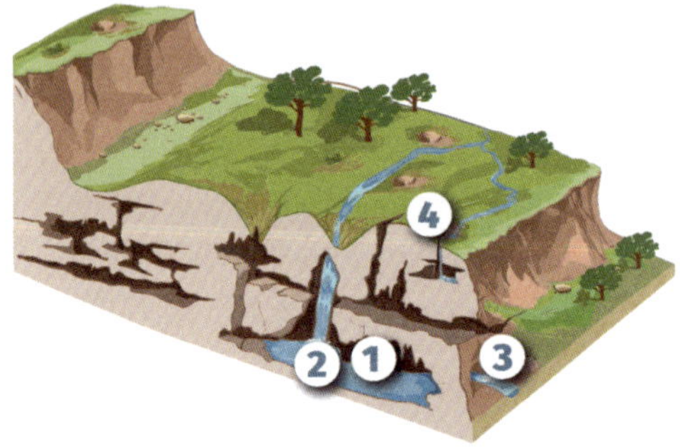

3 Karst spring 4 Doline

DISSOLUTION AND PRECIPITATION

The dissolving effect of the water deepens the **grooves** on the limestone surfaces. If this phenomenon is observed over a larger area, it is called **"Devil's plough"** (a limestone pavement). Bowl-shaped, round depressions are called **sinkholes** (dolines), which range in diameter from a few metres to several hundred metres and can be 50-60 metres deep. When sinkholes connect with each other, an **uvala** is formed. Large basins of the limestone areas are called **polje**. Funnel-shaped depressions are sinkholes whose function is to drain the water collected on the surface into the deeper soil layers. Sinkholes form systems of dissolved karst channels that can expand into caves. **Stalactites** (hanging stones) and **stalagmites** (standing stones) also form in the caves due to the precipitation of calcium carbonate dissolved in the karst water.

INTERESTING FACTS

- *The name karst comes from the name of the Karst Mountains in Slovenia.*
- *Very pure karst water is an important source of drinking water worldwide.*
- *Salt stalactites form from supersaturated brine solutions in salt mines.*

TEST YOUR KNOWLEDGE

1. True or false?

a) The name karst comes from the name of the Karst Mountains in Slovenia.
b) Karst water is heavily polluted and unsuitable for human consumption.
c) In salt mines, salt stalactites can form from supersaturated salt solutions.
d) Another name for stalactite is stalagmite.

2) Match the terms with the definitions.
polje, sinkhole, Devil's plough, doline

a) Large grooves in limestone surfaces.
b) Bowl-shaped depressions in limestone hills.
c) Basins in limestone mountains / hills.
d) Funnel-shaped depression.

8 COLD, SLIGHTLY WARM, HOT!

The climate is divided into zones because – due to the approximately spherical shape of the Earth – the Sun's rays heat different parts of our planet differently. Other factors also affect the climate in the solar zones.

SOLAR CLIMATE ZONES

The further one moves from the Equator towards the pole, the less the angle of inclination of solar radiation, and so decreases its warming effects. The Sun's rays reach the Earth's surface at the smallest angle between the poles and the polar circle, providing little warming effect here. The solar **cold zone** predominates in these areas. The area between the Tropic of Cancer and the Tropic of Capricorn receives the greatest amount of radiation. The solar hot or **tropical zone** forms between the two tropics. Between the tropics and the Arctic Circle, the solar temperate zone is formed. It is a transition between the cold and hot zones.

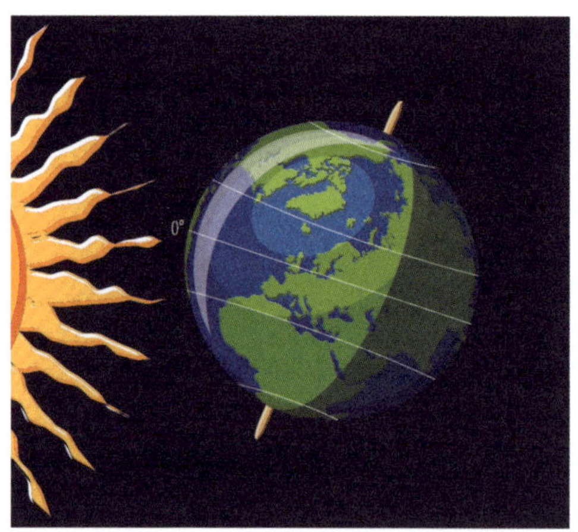

DID YOU KNOW?

Vertical geographical zoning describes how natural conditions vary with altitude in mountainous regions.

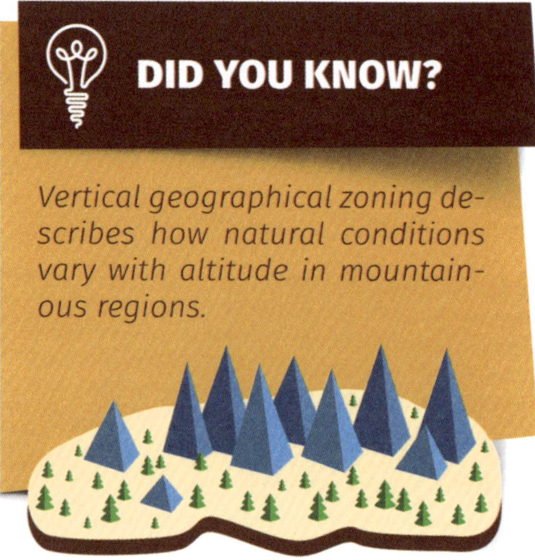

REAL CLIMATE ZONES

Real climate zones are the result of **a variety of factors**. Geographical zonality is the zonal combination of climate, natural vegetation, fauna, soil, and the forces that shape the surface. Within geographical zones, we distinguish belts and within these belts, regions or areas.

TEST YOUR KNOWLEDGE

1. True or false?

a) The Sun's rays reach the surface of the Earth at the smallest angle of inclination between the poles and the Arctic Circle.
b) The area between the Tropic of Cancer and the Tropic of Capricorn receives the greatest amount of radiation.
c) The solar hot or tropical zone forms between the two tropics.
d) The solar temperate zone is formed in the area between the Tropic of Cancer and the Tropic of Capricorn.

2) Match the solar zones with the descriptions.

The area between the Tropic of Cancer and the Tropic of Capricorn.
The area between the poles and the polar circles.
The area between the tropics and the polar circles.

temperate zone
hot zone
cold zone

3) Write the important latitudes on the globe.

- Equator
- Arctic Circle
- Antarctic Circle
- Tropic of Cancer
- Tropic of Capricorn

9

CLIMBING THROUGH CLIMATES!

In mountainous areas, the temperature, pressure, and oxygen content of the air decrease with increasing altitude, while precipitation, daily heat fluctuations, and solar irradiance increase.

ALTITUDINAL ZONES

In **mountain regions**, temperatures are lower all year round, and the annual rainfall is high. With increasing altitudes, corresponding climate zones form. Climatically adapted vegetation demonstrates the **levelling** process.

WHERE ARE THE BOUNDARIES?

One of the most important boundaries separating the zones is the **forest boundary**; there is no contiguous forest above it. The upper limit of solitary trees is marked by the **tree line**. Above the **snow line** is the realm of eternal snow. Between the tree line and the snow line lies the **frost line**.

THE MOUNTAINS OF THE TEMPERATE ZONE

The altitudinal belts of the temperate zone are well illustrated by the **Alps**. Between 500-800 metres, the **typical vegetation** is deciduous forest. Up to 1500 m, beech and pine forests are characteristic, followed by pine forests with dwarf shrubs and rhododendrons. Above the forest boundary (timberline / tree line), dwarf shrubs, mosses and lichens occur up to 2800 m, where the realm of eternal frost begins.

THE TROPICAL ZONE

The altitudinal belts of the mountain ranges of the tropical zone are illustrated by the **Andes** with one of the most complete set of zones.

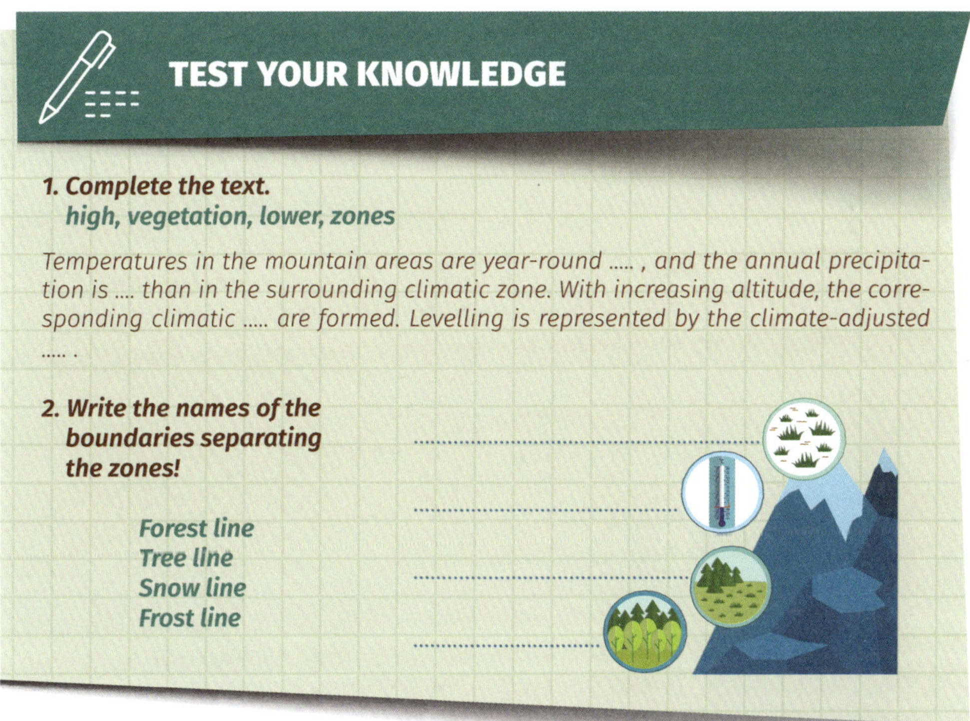

TEST YOUR KNOWLEDGE

1. Complete the text.
high, vegetation, lower, zones

Temperatures in the mountain areas are year-round ..... , and the annual precipitation is .... than in the surrounding climatic zone. With increasing altitude, the corresponding climatic ..... are formed. Levelling is represented by the climate-adjusted ..... .

2. Write the names of the boundaries separating the zones!

Forest line
Tree line
Snow line
Frost line

....

....

....

....

10

WIND IN THE SKY

If the Earth did not rotate on its axis, the warm air from the equator would rise and flow to the poles. It would cool down there and return to the Equator, circulating between the poles and the Equator. However, because it does rotate on its axis, the air is deflected to the right in the Northern Hemisphere and to the left in the Southern Hemisphere as a result of the Coriolis force.

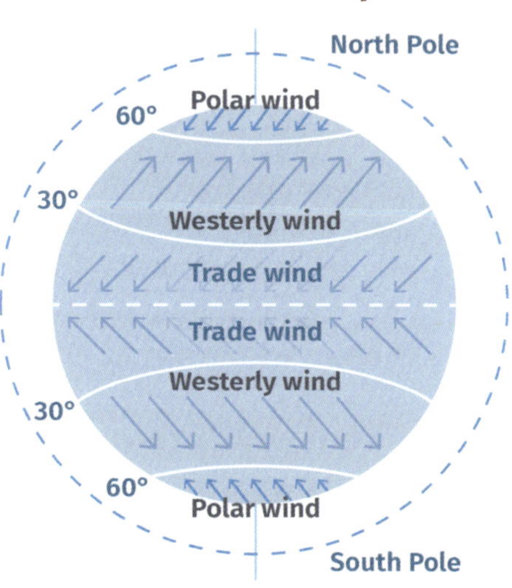

AIR PRESSURE, AIR FLOW

Due to the **different degrees of warming**, a low-pressure belt forms around the Equator and a high-pressure belt forms in the polar regions. The wind systems forming between the different pressure belts are the westerly winds, trade winds and polar winds.

TYPES OF WINDS

Westerly winds (westerlies) are winds in the upper troposphere that move from west to east at speeds of 300-500 km/h. They become saturated with water vapour from the oceans and irrigate the western coasts of the continents with rainfall. The constantly fast **trade winds** ensure the exchange of air between the high-pressure belt along the 30th parallels of latitude and the low-pressure belt along the equator. **Polar winds** (polar easterlies) are typical of the Arctic and Antarctic regions. Polar anticyclones are created by the cooling of surface layers of air. The cold airflow from them is diverted by the Coriolis force.

MONSOON WINDSYSTEM

A monsoon is a surface wind system that changes direction seasonally. The tropical monsoon is caused by the migration of the thermal equator, while the temperate monsoon is caused by the differential warming of land and sea.

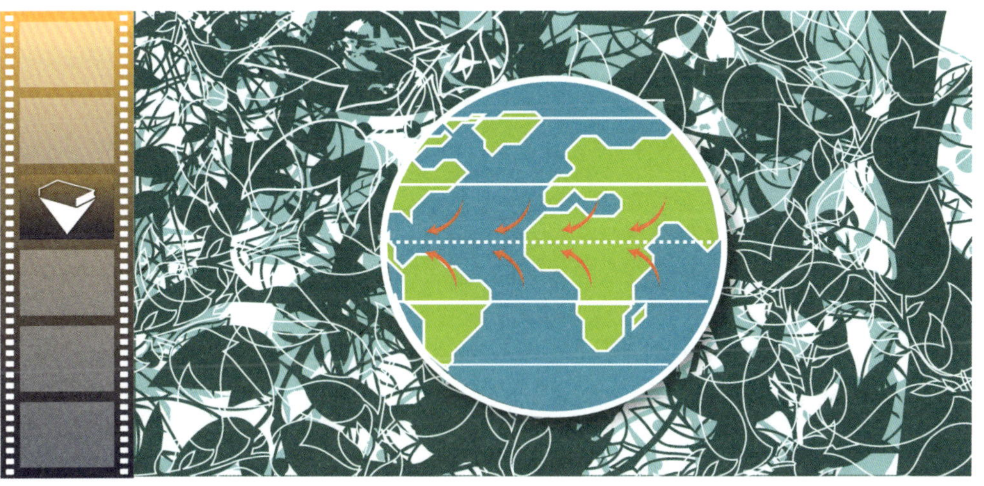

TEST YOUR KNOWLEDGE

1. Match the terms with the definitions.
westerly winds, monsoon, Coriolis force, polar winds

a) The deflecting force due to the Earth's rotation.
b) A near-surface wind system that changes direction seasonally.
c) Winds specific to the Arctic and Antarctic regions.
d) Winds that move from west to east in the upper troposphere.

2. True or false?

a) If the Earth did not rotate, the air would flow from the Equator to the poles.
b) The path of flowing air is changed by the deflecting force of the Earth's rotation.
c) A belt of high air pressure forms around the Equator.
d) The trade winds are constantly moving at low speed.
e) The westerly winds saturated with water vapour from the oceans irrigate the eastern coasts of the continents with precipitation.

11

WEATHER FRONTS

Cyclones are vortices created at the meeting points of cold and warm air masses. They have diameters of thousands of kilometres and travel at high speeds. The meeting points of cold and warm air masses are where fronts form.

WHAT CAUSES THE WIND TO BLOW?

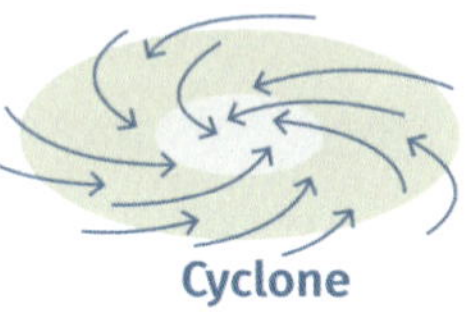
Cyclone

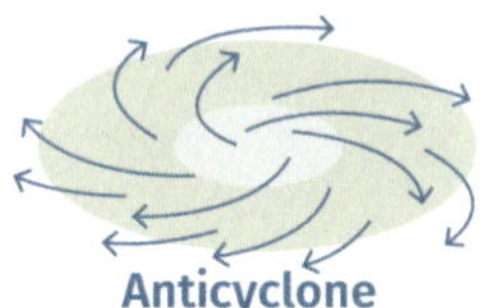
Anticyclone

As the Earth's surface heats up to different degrees, **high and low pressure areas** form. Air always flows from a place of higher pressure to a place of lower pressure. Wind is the movement of air parallel to the surface. The greater the difference in air pressure between two areas is, the higher the wind speed.

CYCLONES, ANTICYCLONES

Cyclones, which move at high speed, form when cold and warm air meet. The air pressure inside them is low, so the air in the middle flows upwards and the air around the cyclone sinks. The swirling spread of air in the high-pressure area creates an **anticyclone**. Inside the anticyclone, the air pressure is high (as opposed to a cyclone), and the air flows outwards.

WHAT IS AIR PRESSURE?

It is the pressure of the air mass on the surface of the Earth and in all directions. Air pressure is measured with a barometer. Its value is influenced by air temperature, latitude and the height above sea level. As you move upwards in the atmosphere, air pressure steadily decreases.

WEATHER FRONTS

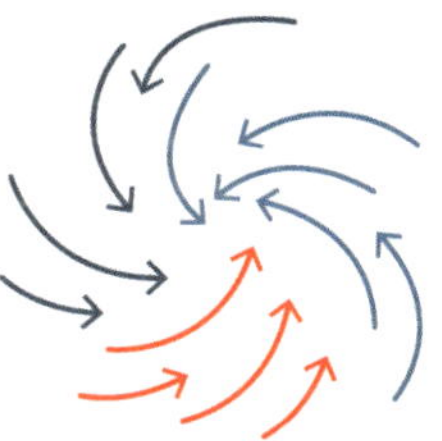

Cyclones are associated with weather fronts, which form in the narrow zone where **warm and cold air mix**. Warm fronts form at the front of cyclones, cold fronts at the back.

TEST YOUR KNOWLEDGE

1. Match the terms with the definitions.
anticyclone, air pressure, wind, cyclones, fronts

a) High-speed vortices with a diameter of thousands of kilometres.
b) They form where cold and warm air masses meet.
c) Air that moves parallel to the surface.
d) It causes sinking air to swirl in an area of high pressure.
e) The pressure of the air mass on the surface of the Earth and in all directions.

2. True or false?

a) In the centre of cyclones, the air flows upwards and sinks around them.
b) Air always flows from higher pressure to lower pressure areas.
c) Weather fronts are cyclone features.
d) Weather fronts form in the narrow zone where warm and cold air mix.

12

MOISTURE IN THE AIR

In the presence of supersaturated air, water vapour condenses on suspended particles of dust or salt crystals forming water droplets. When condensation occurs in higher layers, it forms clouds.

HUMIDITY

The amount of water vapour in the atmosphere is given in g/cm^3. The amount of water vapour per unit volume of air is the **absolute** (actual) **humidity**. The higher the air temperature is, the more moisture it can hold. When it cannot absorb any more water vapour at a certain temperature, it is saturated.

DEW POINT

Dew point is the temperature at which **the air can no longer absorb water vapour**. Air can become saturated in two ways: either it cools below the dew point or it absorbs additional moisture up to the saturation point of the given temperature.

DID YOU KNOW?

Relative humidity expresses the percentage of the water vapour in the air compared to the maximum moisture capacity at that temperature.

PRECIPITATION FORMATION

When the air outside is supersaturated with water vapour, cloud or fog formation begins. The water vapour precipitates onto dust particles, salt crystals, or other impurities, called **condensation nuclei**, on which the water vapour later condenses into water droplets. If the precipitation takes place in layers of air near the ground, fog forms; in higher layers, clouds form. **Condensation** can also occur on the surface of bodies near the ground. For example, ground precipitation is dew, frost, or hoar frost.

TEST YOUR KNOWLEDGE

1. *Match the terms with the definitions.*
condensation nuclei, dew point, absolute humidity, dew

a) Precipitation on the ground.
b) The temperature at which the air becomes saturated.
c) The amount of water vapour per unit volume of air.
d) Dust particles, salt crystals or other impurities on which water vapour precipitates.

13 THE SOURCE OF LIFE

Without water, life on Earth is unimaginable. Water is an essential substance for plants and animals as well. Water and the minerals dissolved in it are also involved in human biochemical processes and thermoregulation.

VITAL WATER

Water is mainly a transport and reaction medium for plants. Most of their nutrients are aqueous solutions absorbed from the soil through their roots. Water seeps into the soil and dissolves soil minerals, inorganic salts, organic matter, gases and pollutants to varying degrees depending on topography, soil moisture content and soil structure. The dissolved ions in soil moisture are surrounded by a **hydration shell**. Precipitation that seeps quickly into dry soils with poor water retention capacity has a low solute content, while water that seeps into moist soils with good water retention capacity has a high **solute content.**

HOW DO ORGANISMS IN WATER SURVIVE THE WINTER?

In winter, the upper layers of natural bodies of water and garden ponds sink when the temperature drops steadily to +4 °C. It is replaced from below by warmer water with lower density. If the water temperature at the surface drops below +4 °C, its density decreases, and it cools further at the surface from top to bottom. Therefore, the resulting ice layer thickens from top to bottom. Below 0 °C, water freezes, its volume increases by 8-10%, thus further decreasing its density, and so ice floats on the surface. Since freezing (or cooling below +4 °C) occurs from top to bottom, the organisms living in the lower layers of the water can survive the winter undisturbed.

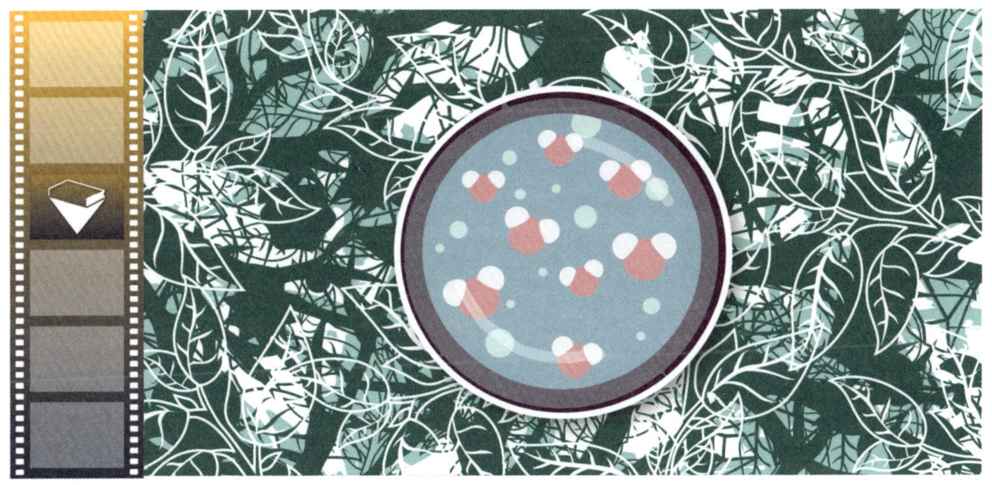

THE CHEMISTRY OF WATER

A water molecule consists of two hydrogen atoms and one oxygen atom, which are connected by a primary polar covalent bond. Chemically pure water is **colourless**, **odourless**, and **tasteless**. At normal atmospheric pressure, it is liquid up to 100 °C, at which temperature it boils. It has its **freezing and melting points at 0 °C**.

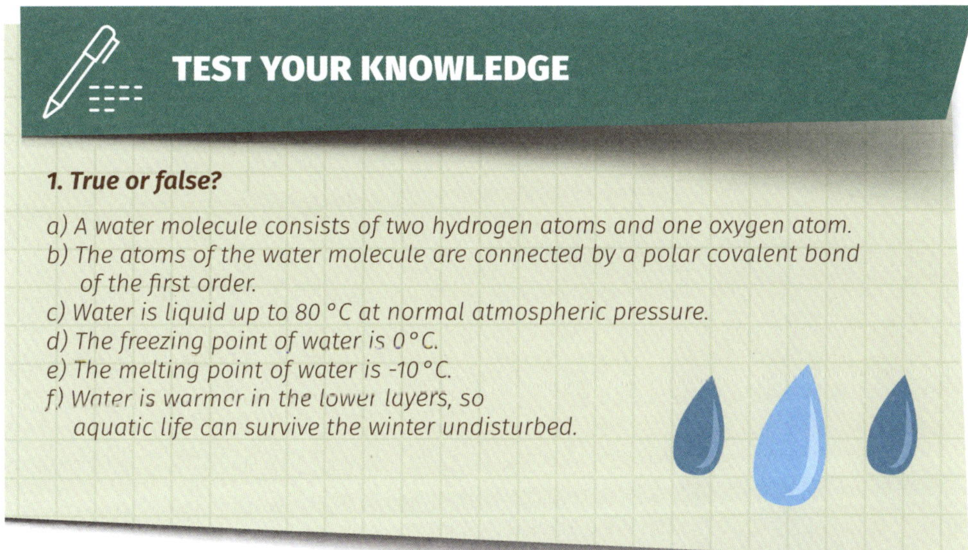

TEST YOUR KNOWLEDGE

1. True or false?

a) A water molecule consists of two hydrogen atoms and one oxygen atom.
b) The atoms of the water molecule are connected by a polar covalent bond of the first order.
c) Water is liquid up to 80 °C at normal atmospheric pressure.
d) The freezing point of water is 0 °C.
e) The melting point of water is -10 °C.
f) Water is warmer in the lower layers, so aquatic life can survive the winter undisturbed.

14

WATER, WATER, EVERYWHERE

The World Ocean, which is made up of seas and oceans, is a continuous body of salt water that covers approximately 71% of the surface of the Earth. In other words, about 361 million km² of it is covered by water.

THE HYDROSPHERE

The total amount of water found on, under, and above the surface of the Earth is called the **hydrosphere**. The constant circulation of water is driven by solar radiation and gravity. The Earth's **water balance** is at equilibrium. The annual amount of precipitation is equal to the annual amount of evaporation. More than 90% of the Earth's total water supply is saline (salt) water and only about 2.7% is freshwater, 80% of which is concentrated in snow and ice layers. The amount of drinking water available to humans is small.

DID YOU KNOW?

Water on Earth is constantly moving. In the atmosphere it takes 9 days for water to renew itself, in the rivers this process takes 11 days, while in the oceans it is very slow; it takes 3450 years.

OCEANS AND SEAS

The oceans, which make up the World Ocean, are large bodies of water in their own basins. Their salinity rarely varies, and their bottom water temperatures are typically 2-3°C. Current systems have developed in the oceans. **The Earth's oceans include the Atlantic, Pacific, Indian, Arctic and Southern Oceans.** The seas are smaller water masses than the oceans. Unlike the oceans, their bottom waters are variable in temperature and salinity. The marginal seas are connected to the oceans. The inland seas are landlocked, connected to the world ocean through narrow channels or straits.

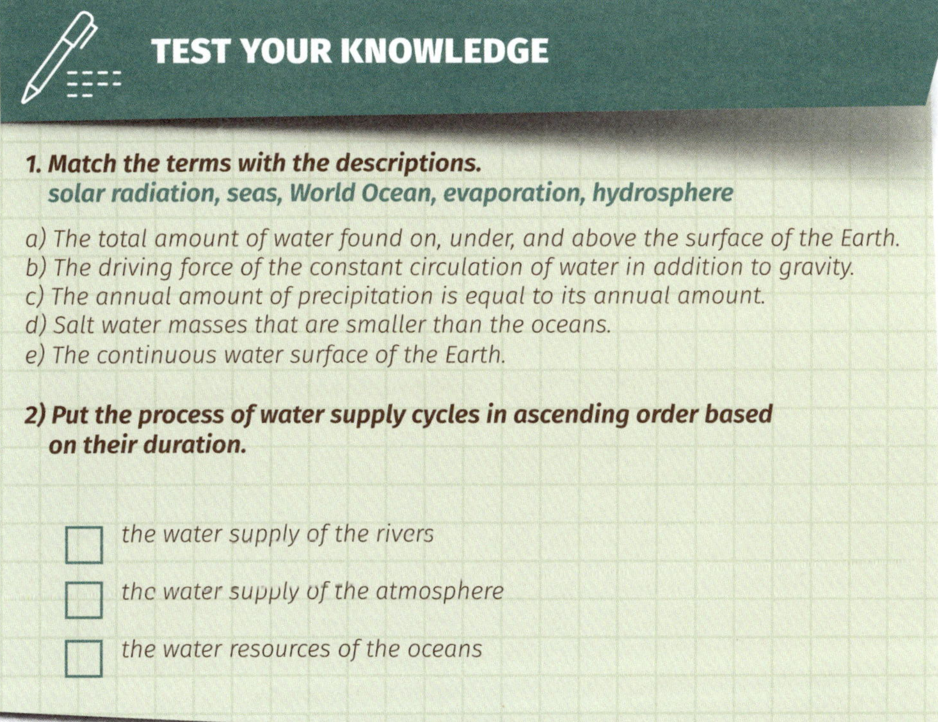

TEST YOUR KNOWLEDGE

1. Match the terms with the descriptions.
solar radiation, seas, World Ocean, evaporation, hydrosphere

a) The total amount of water found on, under, and above the surface of the Earth.
b) The driving force of the constant circulation of water in addition to gravity.
c) The annual amount of precipitation is equal to its annual amount.
d) Salt water masses that are smaller than the oceans.
e) The continuous water surface of the Earth.

2) Put the process of water supply cycles in ascending order based on their duration.

☐ *the water supply of the rivers*

☐ *the water supply of the atmosphere*

☐ *the water resources of the oceans*

15

THE WATER CYCLE

The hydrological cycle, the natural circulation of water is generated by solar radiation and influenced by atmospheric conditions, soil structure, topography, and biome.

A CONSTANT PROCESS

Water is in a constant cycle in nature. The amount of **water that evaporates and runs off** each year is in **equilibrium**. The majority of water molecules are released into the atmosphere through the evaporation of surface water. Evaporation is a process that increases volume. In response to heat, some hydrogen bonds are broken, and water molecules on the surface escape to become water vapour. The humidity in the atmosphere is also influenced by evaporation from living organisms and human activities. Water vapour settles as a result of pressure and temperature changes, and clouds form through condensation. The precipitation that falls from the clouds also dissolves and carries small amounts of pollutants from the air.

FAST / SLOW?

*The hydrological cycle of surface water can be rapid, taking less than a day, while groundwater can remain intact for thousands of years before being returned to the cycle. Water that has already been in the cycle at least once is called **vadose water**, while water that is freshly introduced into the cycle, e.g. through volcanic weathering, is called **juvenile or magmatic water**.*

IN WATER, IN SOIL

Some precipitation is **stored** as snow and ice. Most of the rainwater reaches surface waters, from which it **evaporates** again or slowly **infiltrates** the deeper soil layers, dissolving minerals, organic matter, gases, and pollutants. The soil moisture provides nourishment for plants and then is transpired due to heat.

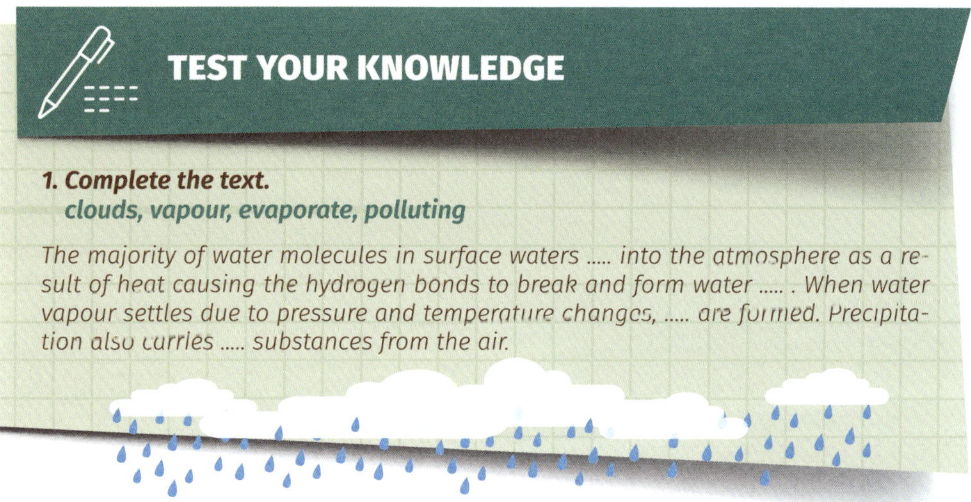

TEST YOUR KNOWLEDGE

1. Complete the text.

clouds, vapour, evaporate, polluting

The majority of water molecules in surface waters ..... into the atmosphere as a result of heat causing the hydrogen bonds to break and form water ..... . When water vapour settles due to pressure and temperature changes, ... are formed. Precipitation also carries ..... substances from the air.

16

SURFACE WATERS

Most of our surface waters – seas and oceans – are made up of salt water, leaving only a minority – lakes, rivers, and polar ice – to be freshwater.

RIVER WATERS

All flowing water comes from springs, which get their water from precipitation, melting snow, and ice. The **water level** of rivers is constantly changing. A **water reservoir** is the area from which the main river with its tributaries collects and drains water. Its boundaries are **watersheds**, consisting of mountains and hills. The areas whose watercourses reach the sea are called drainage areas. In areas without drainage (e.g. the Sahara), the collected water does not reach the seas and oceans. **The 5 longest rivers in the world** include the Nile, the Amazon River, the Yangtze, the Mississippi River, and the Yenisei.

LAKES

Lakes are standing, open bodies of water that form in depressions of the Earth's surface and are fed by precipitation, rising springs, or rivers. **Crater lakes** form in the craters of extinct volcanoes. In the high mountains, the clear standing waters from glacial melt from **mountain lakes or tarns**.

BASIC TERMS RELATED TO WATER

- *Watercourse includes all the surface water bodies in an area.*
- *Water yield is the amount of water that flows through the cross-section of a riverbed in one second.*
- *The fluctuation of the water level of a river is the water flow regime.*
- *The water level of rivers is constantly changing.*
- *A flood is when the water rises over its banks and flows onto the surrounding land.*

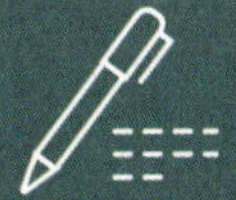

TEST YOUR KNOWLEDGE

1. Match the terms with the definitions.

water level, water flow regime, flood, watercourse, water yield

a) The sum of the surface waters of an area.
b) The amount of water that flows through the cross-section of a river bed in 1 second.
c) The change in the water level of a river.
d) What happens when the river leaves its bed?
e) The height of the water in a river.

17 UNDER THE SURFACE...

Groundwater is rainwater that seeps deep into the ground and is stored in soil, sand and rock. Groundwater plays an important role in the drinking water supply.

WATER EVERYWHERE

Some rainwater infiltrates the ground and then collects above the first impermeable layer or confining bed. This **groundwater** is contaminated and not suitable for human consumption. Fissure water, such as crystal clear **karst water**, fills cracks in the rock. Even a single karst source can provide drinking water for several communities. **Soil moisture** is the water that surrounds soil particles in the form of membranes. The water in an aquifer between two confining beds forced to reach the surface by pressure is called **artesian water**. When its temperature exceeds 20-25 °C, it is called **thermal water**.

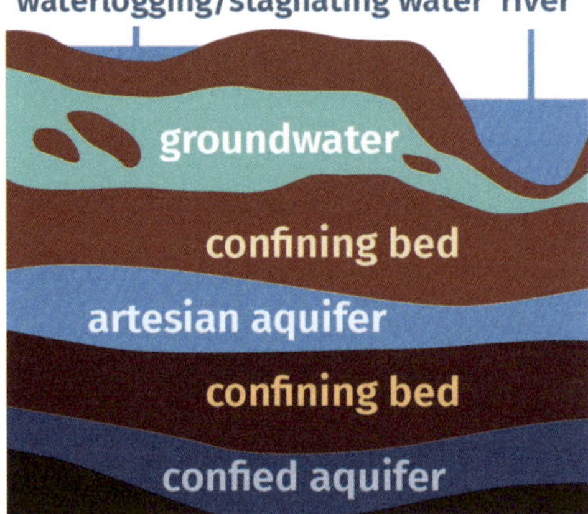

THE FLOODING OF THE GROUNDWATER

After prolonged rainfall or snowfall, the groundwater level rises above the surface. This is called waterlogging (stagnating water), and it has many negative impacts on agriculture.

NATURAL MINERAL WATER

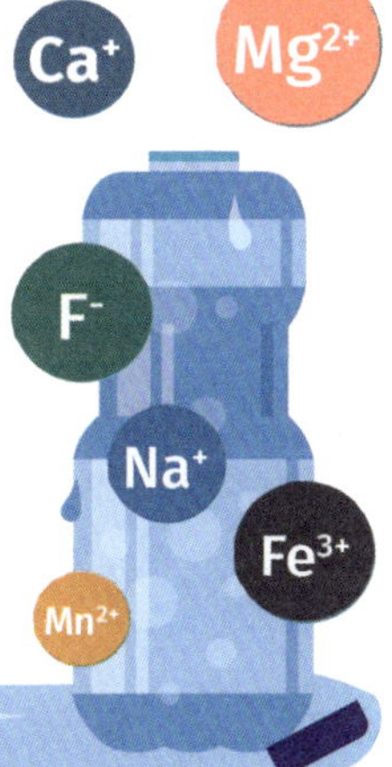

Mineral water is water that has been tested by the health authority, contains no added substances other than carbon dioxide and is free of all impurities and pollutants because it comes from a protected aquifer. Its composition is constant within a deposit. **Spring water** is of the same quality as mineral water, only the content of dissolved substances differs. **Medicinal water** is natural mineral water with a high mineral content and proven medicinal healing properties.

TEST YOUR KNOWLEDGE

1. Match the terms with the descriptions.
artesian water, thermal water, soil moisture, mineral water

a) Water surrounding soil particles in a membrane-like layer.
b) Water between two confining beds.
c) Confined aquifer with a temperature above 20-25 °C.
d) Water tested by a health authority and originating from a protected aquifer or well. It has a constant composition from site to site.

18

ATOMIC MODELS

Throughout the ages scientists have been trying to find out what matter is made up of. In the 5th century BC, some Greek philosophers assumed that matter was made up of tiny particles, which they called atoms.

EARLY ATOMIC THEORIES

According to the theory of the main representative of the atomic theory, **Democritus**, a Greek philosopher in 400 B.C, all matter is composed of tiny particles called atoms. Although these atoms are quantitatively identical, their shape and size are different, resulting in different materials. As an illustration: sweet substances may show spherical shapes, while those of pungent substances may be pointed.

WHAT DOES THE WORD ATOM MEAN?

The Greek word "atomos" means **"uncuttable"**, implying that atoms are the smallest units of matter. We know today that atoms are neutral particles that have charged subatomic building blocks: a positively charged nucleus consisting of positive protons and neutral neutrons. The nucleus is surrounded by a cloud of negatively charged particles, the electrons.

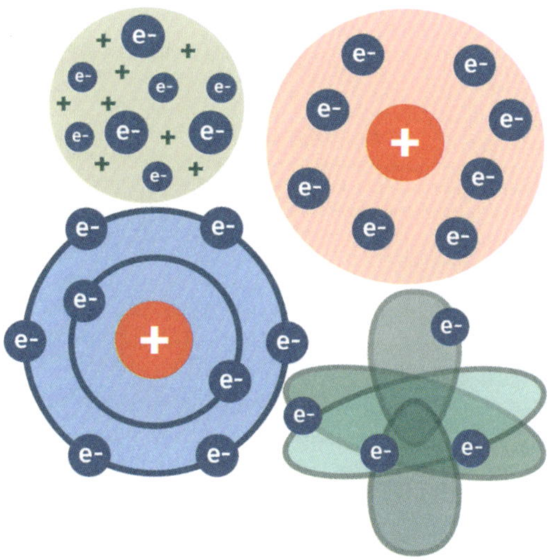

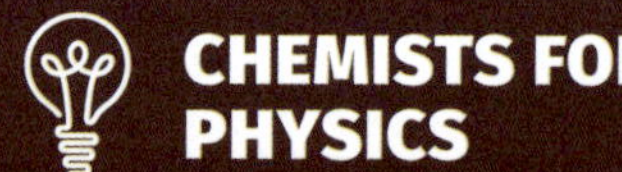

CHEMISTS FOR PHYSICS

At the end of the 18th century, the development of chemistry contributed to a better understanding of atoms. The work of two French chemists, ***Antoine Lavoisier*** *(1743-1794) and* ***Joseph Louis Proust*** *(1754-1826), had the greatest impact.*

MODERN ATOMIC THEORY

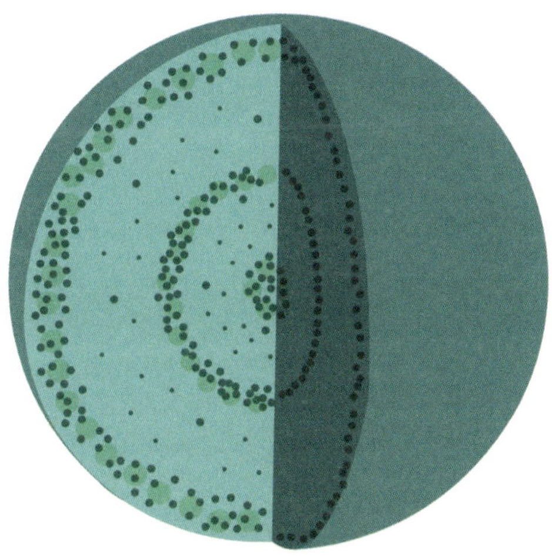

The foundations of today's atomic model were laid out by the physicist **Erwin Schrödinger** (1887-1961) through quantum mechanical calculations. He found that electrons move in energetically-defined orbitals around the nucleus. An electron orbital is defined as the area of space where there is at least a 90% probability of an electron residing.

TEST YOUR KNOWLEDGE

1. Match the names with the facts.
Becquerel, Dalton, Thomson

a) He dusted off the theory of Democritus. He also visualized the particles that make up matter as solid, indivisible spheres.
b) He discovered the electron.
c) He happened to notice that the atoms of certain substances emit invisible radiation.

19 INSIDE THE ATOM

What does an atom look like from the inside? Like an inflated balloon? The universe in miniature? An atom consists of a nucleus and a cloud of electrons surrounding it. It looks like an onion.

THE ATOMIC NUCLEUS

The **two main components of an atom** are the **nucleus** and the **electron cloud**. The atomic nucleus consists of protons and neutrons. Protons are positively charched, while neutrons are neutral. Their masses are almost equal and significant for their size. There is a strong interaction between the particles inside the nucleus. The diameter of the nucleus is one hundred thousandth of the diameter of the atom.

Electron
Proton
Neutron

NEGATIVE CLOUD

Small, light **electrons move in atomic orbitals** around the nucleus. Their mass is only two thousandths of that of a proton. Negatively charged electrons remain close to the nucleus because of an electrical attraction. The number of electrons in each atom is equal to the number of protons, therefore the atom is neutrally charged.

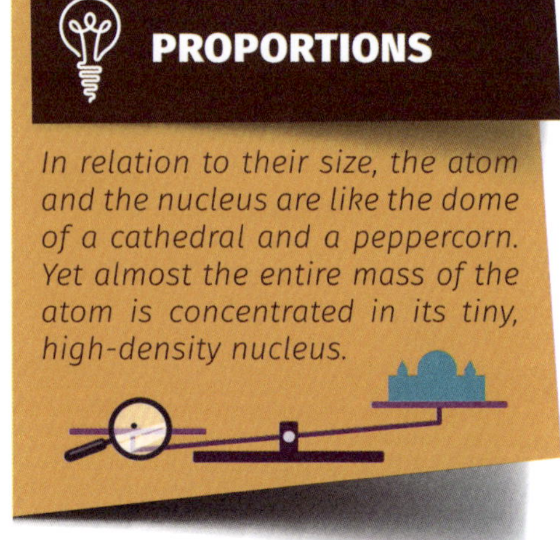

PROPORTIONS

In relation to their size, the atom and the nucleus are like the dome of a cathedral and a peppercorn. Yet almost the entire mass of the atom is concentrated in its tiny, high-density nucleus.

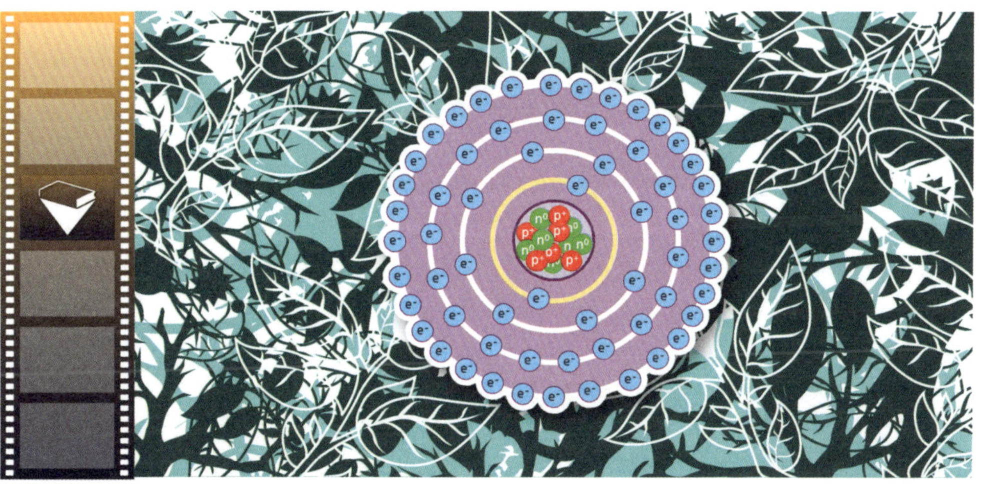

TEST YOUR KNOWLEDGE

1. *Match the terms to the descriptions.*
valence shell, first shell, nucleus, oxygen

a) It is composed of positively charged protons and neutral neutrons.
b) Its electron shell consists of eight electrons.
c) The outermost electron shell is also called this.
d) This shell can have up to two electrons.

2. True or false?

a) A positively charged nucleus attracts negatively charged electrons.
b) The electron cloud is composed of negatively charged electrons.
c) Particles with the same charge attract each other.
d) Almost the entire mass of the atom is concentrated in its nucleus.
e) The mass of an electron is only one hundredth of the mass of a proton.
f) The electrons on the valence shell are involved in chemical reactions.

20 THE WORLD'S COMPOSITION

The materials that make up our world can be very different depending on the particles they are composed of. Simple substances cannot be broken down into further substances by chemical reactions.

ELEMENTS

Simple substances are called **elements**. Elements are the building blocks for other substances. The particles that make up the elements are called atoms.

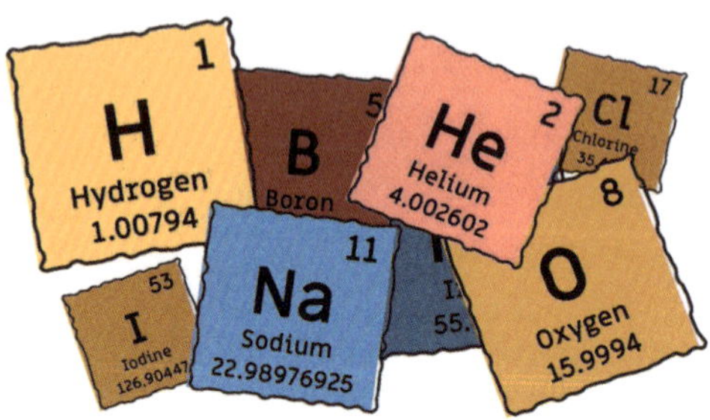

THE PERIODIC TABLE OF ELEMENTS

Different elements have different particle structures and different properties. For example, they can have different colours, different states of matter or different behaviour towards air, or water. However, there are similarities between certain elements. The **periodic table** is a summary table of the isolated elements discovered so far. In this system, the elements are represented by a 1, 2 or 3 letter abbreviation formed from their names, called a chemical symbol.

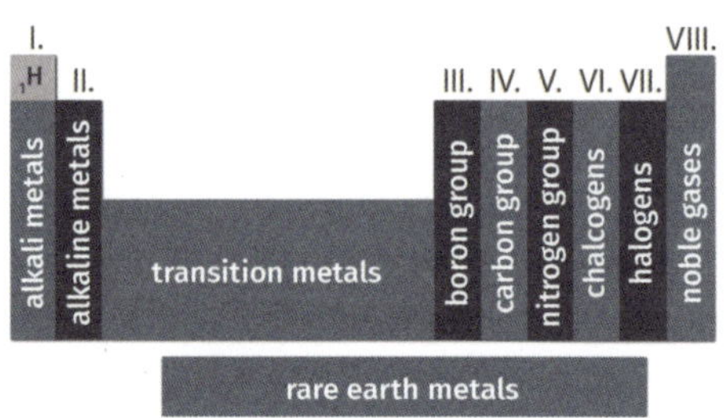

PERIODIC TABLE

*The first version was created by the Russian chemist **Mendeleev**. The scientist grouped the 60 chemical elements known at the time according to their recurring, i.e. periodic, chemical properties.*

Dmitri Ivanovich Mendeleev

THE FORMATION AND DECAY OF ELEMENTS

Enormous amounts of energy are needed to produce the elements, i.e. for **nucleosynthesis**. Stars in space are such **"element furnaces"** in which elements are created through various **nuclear reactions**. Elements cannot be broken down further by chemical reactions, but using nuclear energy they can be.

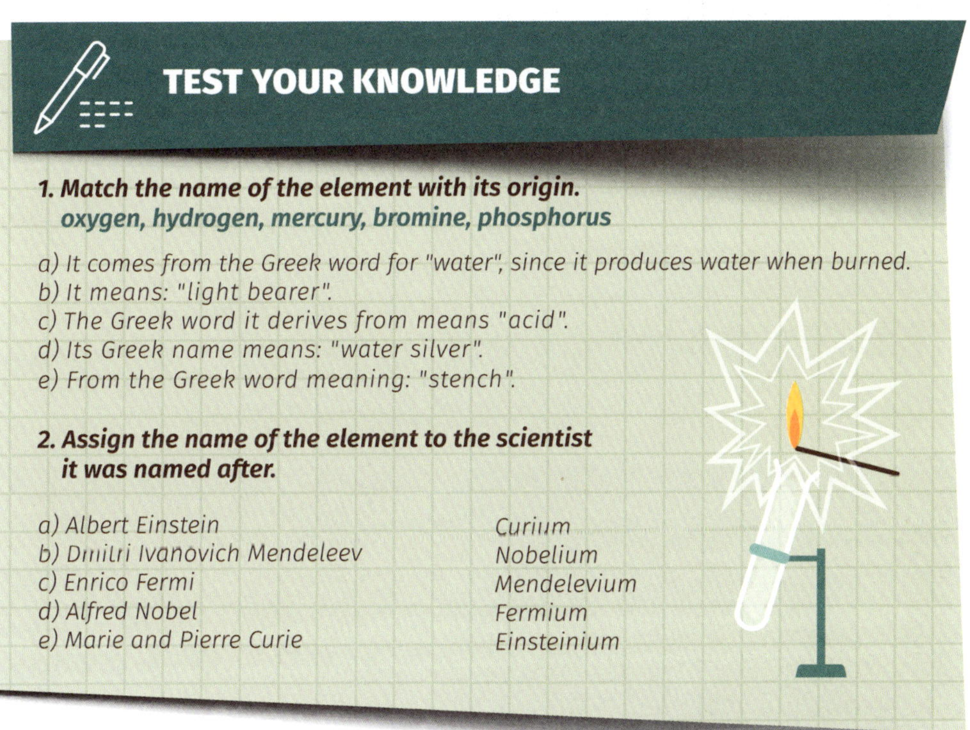

TEST YOUR KNOWLEDGE

1. Match the name of the element with its origin.
oxygen, hydrogen, mercury, bromine, phosphorus

a) It comes from the Greek word for "water", since it produces water when burned.
b) It means: "light bearer".
c) The Greek word it derives from means "acid".
d) Its Greek name means: "water silver".
e) From the Greek word meaning: "stench".

2. Assign the name of the element to the scientist it was named after.

a) Albert Einstein	*Curium*
b) Dmitri Ivanovich Mendeleev	*Nobelium*
c) Enrico Fermi	*Mendelevium*
d) Alfred Nobel	*Fermium*
e) Marie and Pierre Curie	*Einsteinium*

21

WHY IS IT THE WAY IT IS?

The materials in nature are diverse. We can see that some materials break or melt easily, while others are almost indestructible. Solid bodies have a crystalline structure.

CRYSTAL LATTICE

The particles of solids are arranged in a **regular three-dimensional lattice**. The lattice points contain atoms, molecules or ions. Based upon the nature of the particles and the types of bonds between them, the types of lattices are atomic, molecular, ionic and metal lattice.

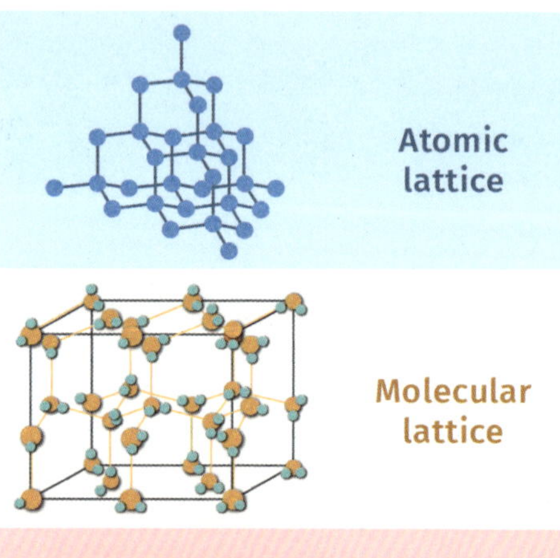

DID YOU KNOW?

Diamond, one of the allotropes of carbon, is the hardest known material. Diamond is made up of an atomic lattice.

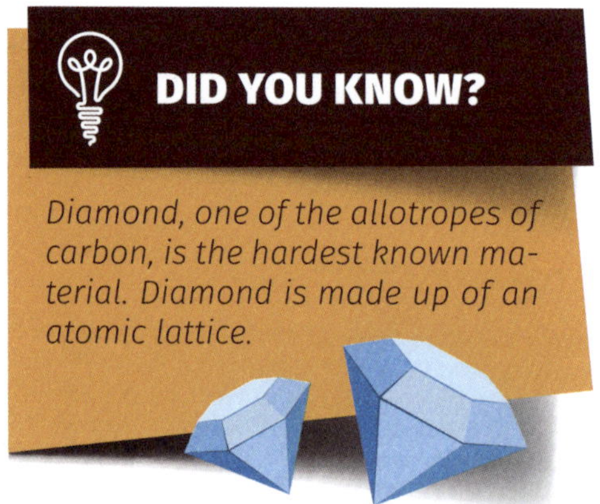

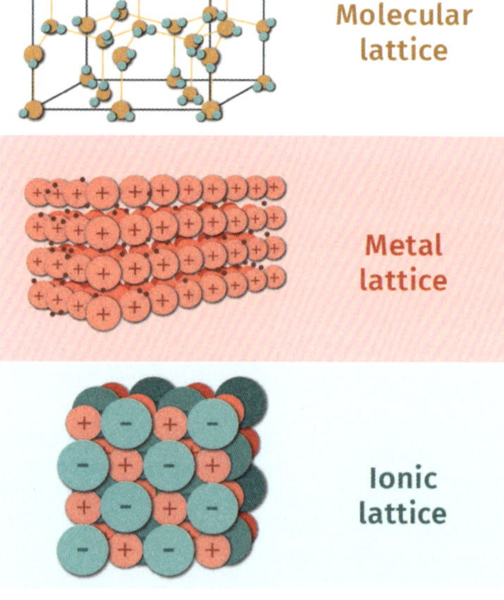

WHAT ARE THE HARDEST SUBSTANCES?

The secret of chemically resistant, hard materials lies in their atomic lattice structure. The atoms at the lattice points of **atomic lattice crystals** are connected by **strong covalent bonds**. This makes them hard and gives them a high melting point. They are poor conductors of both heat and electricity. They are neither soluble in water nor in organic solvents.

METAL LATTICE MATERIALS

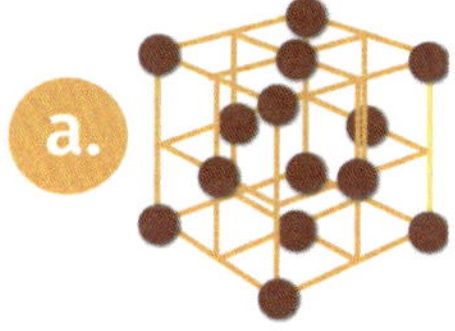

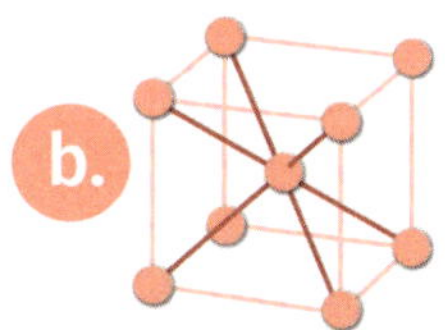

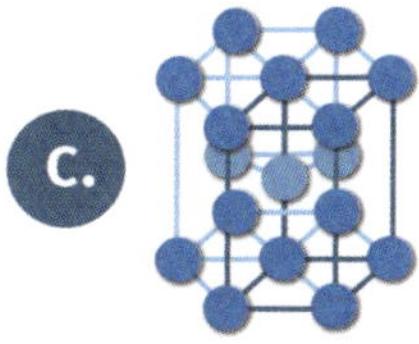

Metal atoms have a few, loosely bound electrons on their outer electron shells, which are easily stripped from the atoms to form **positive metal ions**. The lattice points of the metal lattice thus contain positive metal ions, while the stripped electrons form a **freely moving electron cloud** that extends across the lattice and holds the positive metal ions together. The metallic bond is a primary bond, which is hard to break. Based on their unit cells, the three basic types of metal lattice are the "face-centred cubic" (fcc) (**a**), the "body-centred cubic" (bcc) (**b**) and the "hexagonal close packed" (hcp) (**c**). Most metals are characterised by good ductility and undergo plastic deformation relatively easily.

TEST YOUR KNOWLEDGE

1. Match the lattice structures to the pictures.
face-centred cubic (fcc) crystal lattice, body-centred cubic (bcc) crystal lattice, hexagonal close packed (hcp) crystal lattice

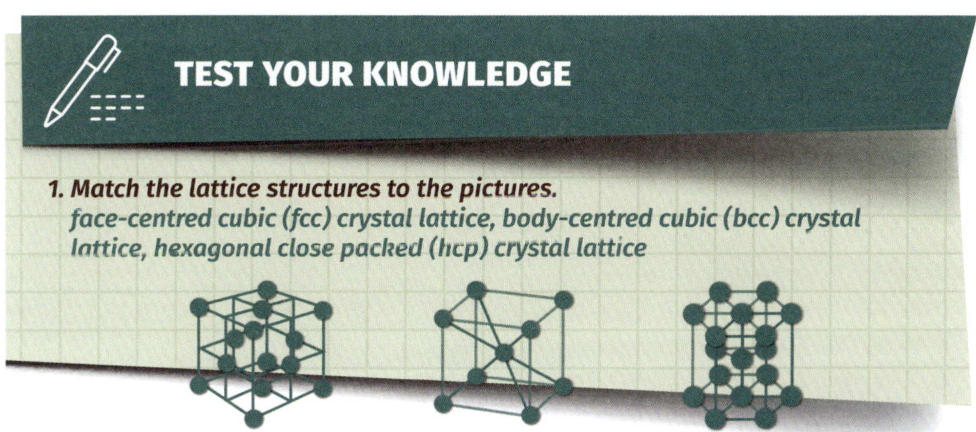

22 BLACK DIAMONDS

Non-renewable energy sources include coal, natural gas and oil. All three were created in a long process from the remains of dead plants and animals over millions of years.

THE FORMATION OF COAL

The formation of black coal begins with the accumulation of dead plant remains from large forests, which are later covered by a layer of sediment. Under the weight of these cover layers, carbon formation begins in an oxygen-free environment, resulting in the accumulation of compounds containing carbon. Coal is classified as **sedimentary rock of organic origin**. Longer coalification, thicker seams and higher pressure yield better quality coal with a higher calorific value. The formation of **brown coal** (**lignite**) takes tens of millions of years, that of **black** (**hard**) **coal** 280-350 million years. If the coalification process takes even longer, anthracite with a carbon content of 92-98 % is produced. Under suitable conditions, **anthracite** turns into graphite.

CARBON FORMATION			
Peat	Lignite	Brown coal	Black coal
Ten thousand years	A few million years	Tens of millions of years	280-350 million years

MINERAL COAL

In nature, the crystalline forms of carbon, diamond and graphite, occur in relatively small quantities. Coal which contains **organic compounds with a high carbon content** besides carbon, is abundant.

PEAT AND LIGNITE

The first step in **coalification** is the formation of peat, in which the plant parts are still visible to the naked eye. **Peat** takes a few tens of thousands of years to form. **Lignite**, which is a few million years old, still contains vaguely visible plant materials.

TEST YOUR KNOWLEDGE

1. Tick the correct statements.

a) The formation of black (hard) coal is associated with dead plant remains.
b) Coal is a sedimentary rock with an organic origin.
c) At higher pressure, coal with a higher calorific value is produced.
d) The first product of carbon formation is lignite.
e) Brown coal still contains plant parts.
f) Parts of plants are still visible in peat.
g) Lignite takes longer to form than black (hard) coal.
h) Black (hard) coal is not a renewable energy source.

2. Write the matching names next to the pictures.

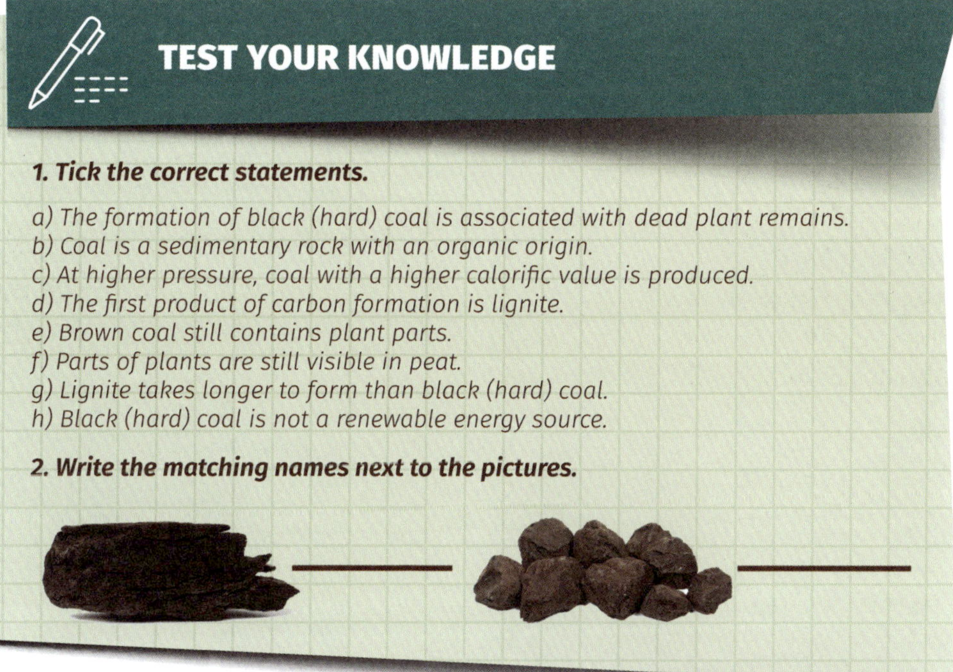

23

TRIPLETS

The three allotropic modifications of carbon are diamond, graphite, and fullerene. The different properties of the allotropes result from their different structures.

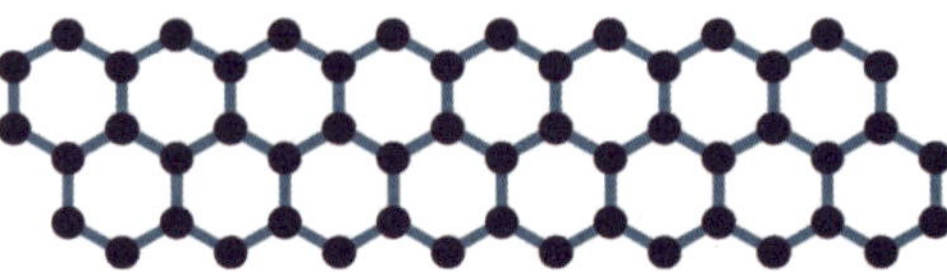

DIAMONDS

Diamond is considered to be the **hardest known naturally occuring mineral** on Earth. It is almost indestructible. Its particles form tetrahedral atomic lattices. Each carbon atom is covalently bonded to four other carbon atoms. Due to its rigid structure, diamond is very hard and has a high melting point. It does not conduct heat or electrical current and has no solvents.

GRAPHITE

Graphite is dark grey, **opaque** and **soft**. In graphite crystals, carbon atoms form layers of hexagonal lattice. Each carbon atom in a plane is covalently bonded to three other carbon atoms. The layers are held together by weaker metallic bonds, which is why graphite is a good conductor of electricity and heat. Because the layers can slide over each other, graphite is suitable for drawing with.

GRAPHENE

A special modification of carbon is the one atom thick layer of graphite, called graphene. It contains a single layer of carbon atoms, tightly bound in a hexagonal honeycomb lattice. It is theoretically possible for carbon to form a giant molecule with an infinite number of atoms in this manner.

EXCITING FULLERENES

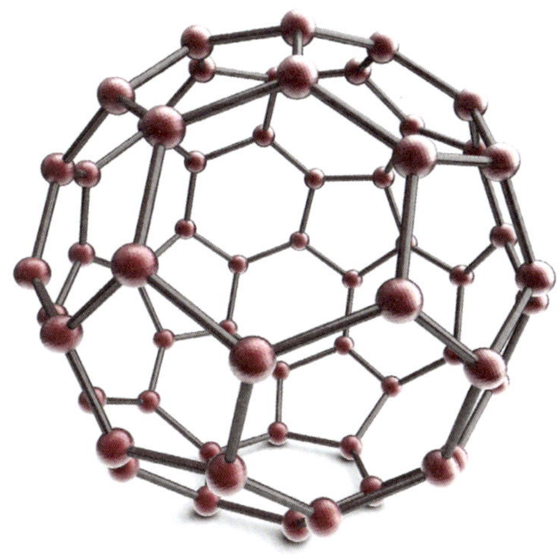

The term fullerene refers to a diverse **family of molecules** with an even number of carbon atoms. Each carbon atom is covalently bonded to three other carbon atoms in an arrangement of five- or six-membered rings. A fullerene molecule is either **spherical**, or resembles a tube made from a **rolled-up mesh sheet**. The perfectly symmetrical C_{60} molecule is extraordinarily stable and its lattice looks like a football.

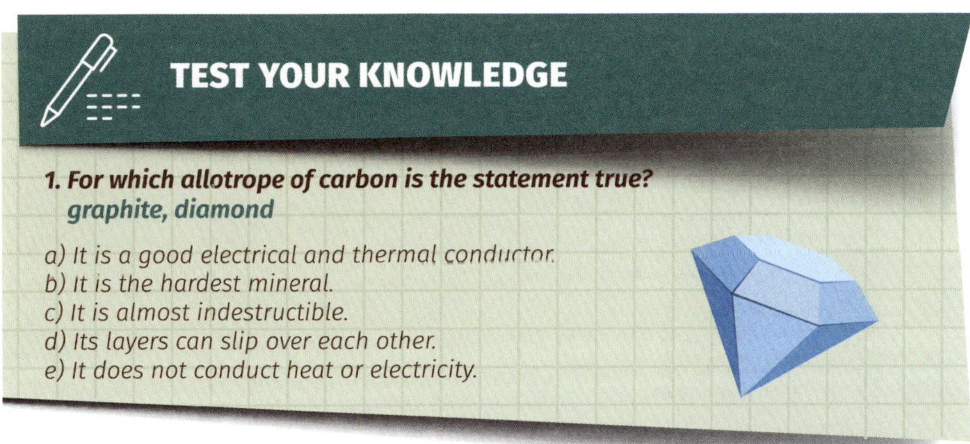

TEST YOUR KNOWLEDGE

1. For which allotrope of carbon is the statement true?
graphite, diamond

a) It is a good electrical and thermal conductor.
b) It is the hardest mineral.
c) It is almost indestructible.
d) Its layers can slip over each other.
e) It does not conduct heat or electricity.

24

SECRET OF THE MINES

Minerals or mineral assemblages that contain a higher than average proportion of a certain type of metal are called ores. Ores are formed by magmatic processes or by sedimentation.

MAGMATIC (IGNEOUS) ORE DEPOSITS

Magmatic ore deposits are formed when during the eruption, the **magma cools** on its way to the surface. Heavy metals (chromium, platinum, nickel, iron), with the highest melting points, are the first to form deposits. Later, they sink to the bottom of the melt and accumulate there. Pushing upwards, the magma residues penetrate the cracks in the host rock, where they cool and form lodes of ore. During cooling, **ores** are precipitated from the gases and vapours of the magma. This is how uranium, tin and thorium deposits are formed.

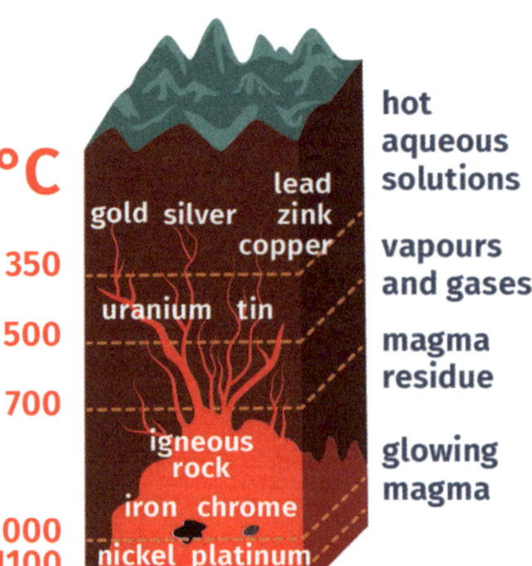

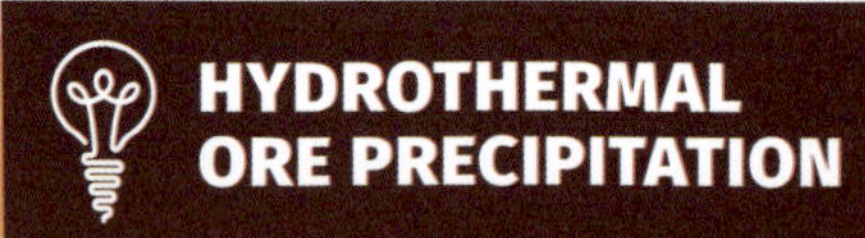

HYDROTHERMAL ORE PRECIPITATION

During hydrothermal ore precipitation, ground water enters the cooling magma, and gets heated up. The hot water leaches metals from the magma as it passes through. The lode deposits of precious and non-ferrous metals (zinc lead, copper) form by precipitation from the hydrothermal fluids.

SEDIMENTARY ORE DEPOSITS

The formation of sedimentary ore deposits begins with the **weathering of rocks**. Ore minerals **are leached** from the pieces by the surface runoff and **precipitate upon** reaching the seawater. Marine organisms play a role in the enrichment of ore deposits. This is how sedimentary manganese, copper, zinc, and iron ore deposits are formed.

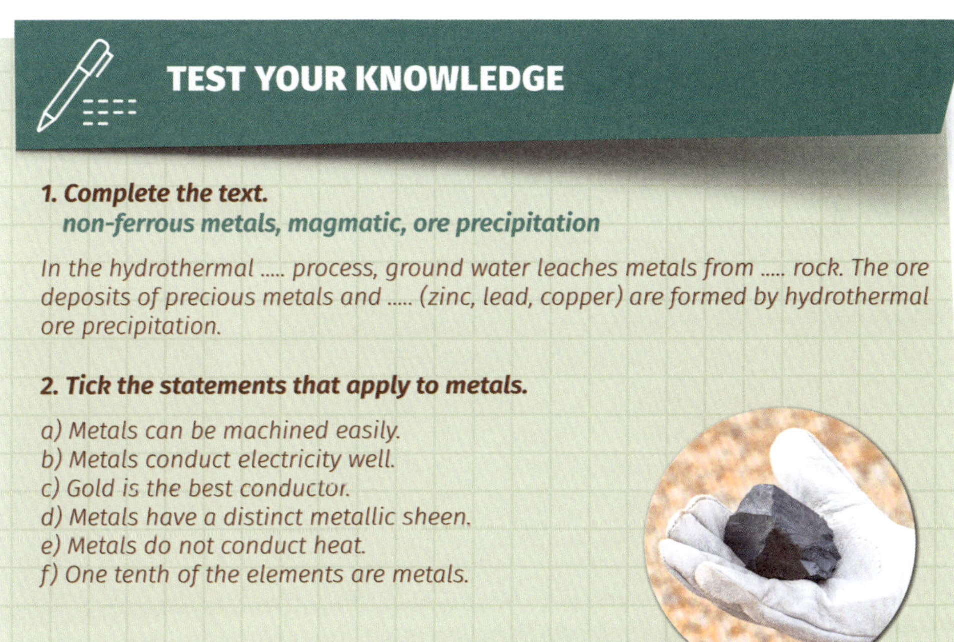

TEST YOUR KNOWLEDGE

1. Complete the text.
non-ferrous metals, magmatic, ore precipitation

In the hydrothermal ..... process, ground water leaches metals from ..... rock. The ore deposits of precious metals and ..... (zinc, lead, copper) are formed by hydrothermal ore precipitation.

2. Tick the statements that apply to metals.

a) Metals can be machined easily.
b) Metals conduct electricity well.
c) Gold is the best conductor.
d) Metals have a distinct metallic sheen.
e) Metals do not conduct heat.
f) One tenth of the elements are metals.

25

SEDIMENTARY ROCKS

Sedimentary rocks cover three quarters of the Earth's surface. They were formed by the external forces of the Earth. Rock-forming processes include fragmentation, weathering, transport, deposition, and lithification.

DETRITAL AND HETEROGENEOUS SEDIMENTARY ROCK

Like igneous rocks, sedimentary rocks are grouped based on their formation. **Detrital (clastic) sedimentary rocks** are formed from the fragmented, transported and eventually deposited debris of older rocks. These include gravel, sand, and sandstone, which consist of cemented sand particles. Marl, clay, and silt are composed of smaller grains. **Heterogeneous sedimentary rock** is bauxite, an important raw material for both alumina and aluminium production.

Heterogeneous sedimentary rock

Detrital sedimentary rocks

CHEMICAL SEDIMENTARY ROCKS

In the formation of chemical sedimentary rocks, chemical weathering plays a role in addition to fragmentation. The size, structure and composition of the rocks change during pysical and chemical weathering. **Evaporites** are chemical sedimentary rocks formed by the evaporation and drying of salt water lakes and seas. The solubility of salts varies, so the less soluble salts precipitate first, before the more soluble ones.

SEDIMENTARY ROCKS OF ORGANIC ORIGIN

Sedimentary rocks of organic origin are formed from the remains of living organisms. One example is **limestone**, which mostly consists of the remains of corals and other calcareous marine organisms. **Carbonaceous rocks** (hard coal, lignite, peat, etc.) and **hydrocarbons** (natural gas, petroleum) also belong to this group.

TEST YOUR KNOWLEDGE

1. Match the sedimentary rock types to the descriptions.
chemical, debris, organic

a) It is formed by the fragmentation, transport and eventual deposition of older rocks.
b) After physical fragmentation, the rock also undergoes a chemical change.
c) It is formed from the dead remains of living organisms.

2. Mark the statements that do not apply to aluminium.

a) Its strength is increased by alloying it with magnesium.
b) It has a silvery colour.
c) It is difficult to work with.
d) Its raw material is bauxite.
e) It is a good thermal and electrical conductor.
f) It is also used in aircraft.

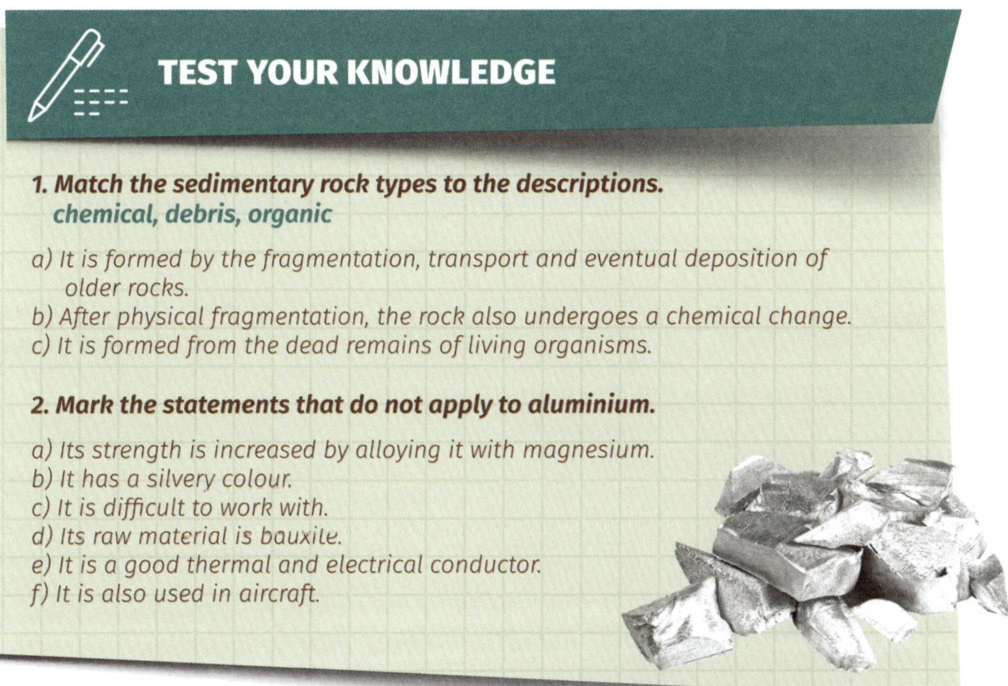

26

STRIKE WHILE IT IS HOT

Iron is one of the oldest known metals, and still one of the most important for mankind. Its atomic number is 26 in the periodic table and its symbol is Fe, which comes from the Latin word "ferrum".

ABOUT IRON

Iron is a grey coloured metal with a high melting point. Above 900°C its crystal structure changes to a face-centred crystal lattice, which is much more malleable than the stable body-centred structure at ordinary temperatures; therefore, it is **forged red-hot**.

REACTIONS OF IRON

Iron reacts with oxygen in the presence of moisture at normal room temperature. The resulting complex **iron (III) oxide-hydroxide** is **rust**, which forms a loose layer on the surface of the iron object. Rust provides no protection from further oxidation, and therefore, objects of iron can disintegrate completely in humid air. At high temperatures, iron powder **burns in a shower of sparks**. At higher temperatures, it also reacts with chlorine to form lemon yellow iron chloride and with sulphur to form iron sulphide.

IRON COMPOUNDS

- **Iron sulphide** is a blackish-grey, brittle, very hard material.
- **Iron disulfide** naturally occurs in the mineral called pyrite. Its beautiful gold-coloured crystals are colloquially known as "fool's gold". It is a raw material for the production of sulphuric acid.
- **Ferrous sulphate**, also known as copperas, forms green crystals that lose water when exposed to air, and turn white. Ferrous sulphate can be safely used in your garden as spray fertilizer.

TEST YOUR KNOWLEDGE

1. *Tick the statements that apply to iron.*

a) One of the oldest mankind.
b) Its atomic number is 26.
c) Its chemical symbol is F.
d) It is a grey metal.
e) It has a high melting point.

2. Match the iron compound to the description.
ferrous sulphate, iron sulphide, Pyrite

a) Blackish-grey, brittle, very hard material
b) Colloquially known as "fool's gold".
c) Also known as copperas. Also used as a spraying agent.

3. True or false?

a) For industrial use, it is extracted from iron ore by reduction.
b) In its pure state, iron has a distinct metallic sheen and a silvery colour
c) Iron is very malleable.
d) Iron is very resistant and is only attacked by nitric acid.
e) Iron is often alloyed with other elements.
f) Pig or crude iron is used as a raw material for steelmaking.
g) Carbon is the most important alloying element of iron.

27

THE QUEEN OF METALS

Silver is a transition metal of the periodic table, with an atomic number of 47. If gold is the king of the precious metals, silver is the queen.

PROPERTIES OF SILVER

The softness of pure silver makes it **easy to work with**, but it has poor wear resistance. In its pure state, it has **excellent electrical and thermal conductivity** and high reflectivity. It is very resistant to chemicals. Its **antiviral** and **antimicrobial** properties make silver effective against lots of different viruses, bacteria, fungi and certain parasites. Certain silver compounds can be found in sprays, creams, ointments, powders, anti-perspirant deodorant sticks, and plasters.

SILVER IN ANTIQUITY...

Even in ancient times, people knew the **beneficial effects** of silver. They kept silver coins in their vessels or stored water in silver jugs and food in silver pots. Later, silver cutlery in Europe and silver chopsticks in China were used by wealthier families.

...AND TODAY

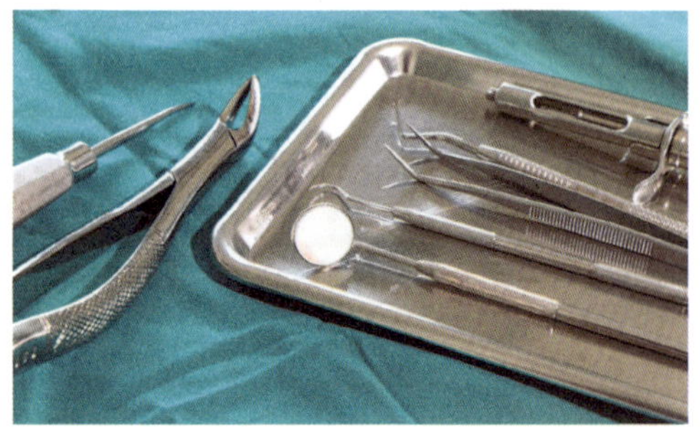

Silver is used as a **disinfectant coating** on cutlery, medical instruments, water treatment equipment, interior coatings and filter inserts for washing machines, dishwashers and refrigerators, and even in toilet seat coatings.

RAINMAKER SILVER

Silver iodide is often used for weather modification applications. Currently, China has the largest cloud seeding system - silver iodide is sprayed on clouds to trigger the formation of raindrops, and to further accelerate cloud formation.

$$Ag^{+} + I^{-} \longrightarrow AgI$$

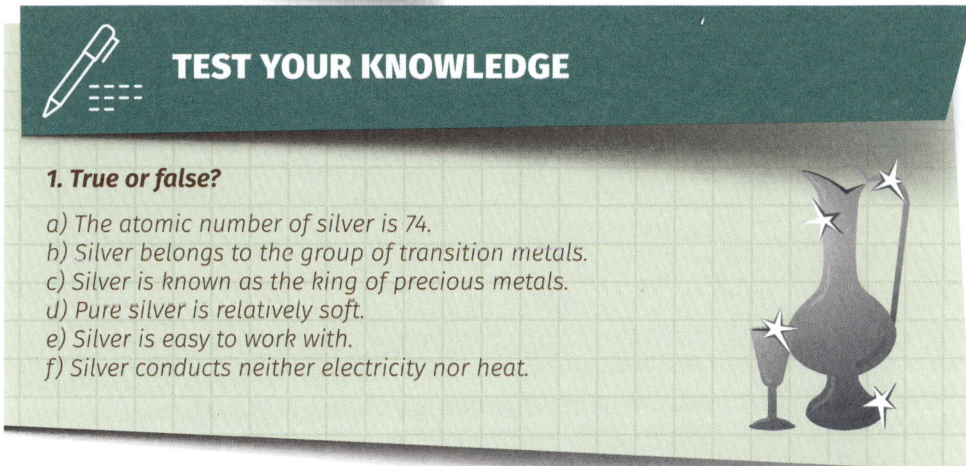

TEST YOUR KNOWLEDGE

1. True or false?

a) The atomic number of silver is 74.
b) Silver belongs to the group of transition metals.
c) Silver is known as the king of precious metals.
d) Pure silver is relatively soft.
e) Silver is easy to work with.
f) Silver conducts neither electricity nor heat.

28 GOLDEN SHINE

Gold is the king of precious metals. It is cherished for its exceptional properties, and has always been a symbol of luxury. It has mostly been the privilege of the wealthy to enjoy its beauty in jewellery and household items.

PRECIOUS METALS

Precious metals are **rare** and **durable**. They have low reactivity, so they retain their luster, colour, and consistence. **Gold, too, is almost indestructible.** It does not oxidise even at high temperatures. It can only be dissolved in a mixture of concentrated nitric and hydrochloric acid, also known as *aqua regia* (latin for "royal water").

GOLD PANNING

Panning for gold has been going on for a long time. **Gold prospectors** extract gold from river sediments by the process of panning. Not all rivers yield gold, only the ones with **gold ore** deposits in their catchment area, as the river water picks up and transports gold particles, large or small, from the source. The panners wash the sediment and the heavier gold particles settle faster than the sand and gravel.

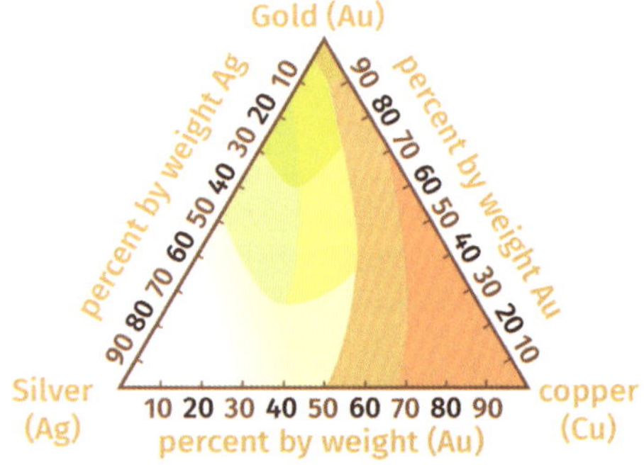

DID YOU KNOW?

All that glitters is not gold... Did you know that the Golden Raspberry Award goes to the worst film in the movie industry?

WHAT IS MADE OF GOLD?

Most gold is used for making **jewellery** and **coins**. Since gold is rather a soft metal, it is usually **alloyed with** silver or copper. Its ability to conduct electricity well makes it an indispensable component of the electronics industry.

TEST YOUR KNOWLEDGE

1. True or false?

a) Precious metals are rare.
b) Precious metals decay relatively quickly.
c) Precious metals are highly reactive.
d) Gold is created in supernova explosions.
e) The amount of gold on our planet is constant.
f) Gold is an extremely hard metal.

2. Choose the correct solution.
What can gold be dissolved in?

- ☐ *Hydrochloric acid*
- ☐ *Aqua regia*
- ☐ *Nitric acid*

29 EXHAUSTIBLE ENERGY RESOURCES

Two of our most important energy sources, oil and natural gas, are both fossil fuels, meaning they formed from the remains of dead plants and animals over millions of years. When they burn, they release a great amount of heat.

CRUDE OIL

Crude oil or petroleum is a dark, opaque liquid with a lower density than water. **It is a mixture of many different compounds.** During the refining process, it is separated into a number of fractions, such as petrol, paraffin, diesel, and asphalt. The entire mixture heated, and the fractions evaporate one-by-one, based on their different boiling points.

NATURAL GAS

In its natural state, natural gas is a colourless, odourless, transparent, water-insoluble **organic gas**, which is lighter than air, and consists of various hydrocarbon compounds. It is extracted by drilling and, after purification, is transported mainly in gaseous form through gas pipelines or, less frequently, in tanker ships or trucks in liquid form. Purified natural gas is delivered to homes in pipes for heating and cooking.

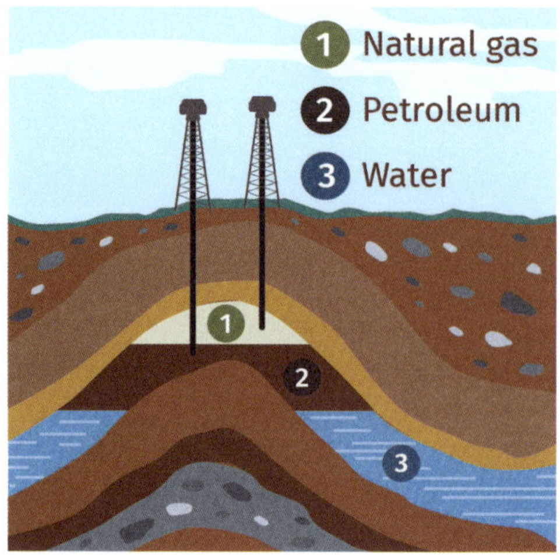

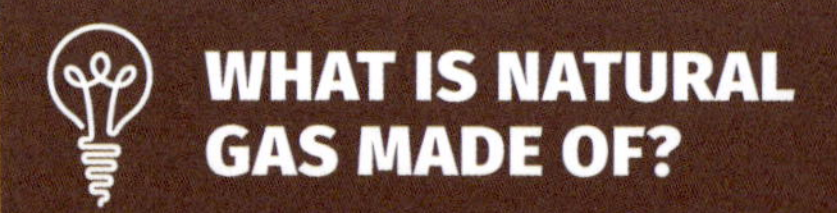

WHAT IS NATURAL GAS MADE OF?

Natural gas is primarily made up of methane and ethane. Two other important components are propane and butane. Depending on where it is mined, natural gas can also contain small amounts of carbon dioxide, oxygen, nitrogen and noble gases, such as: argon, helium, neon or xenon.

LPG (LIQUEFIED PETROLEUM GAS)

In everyday use, a **mixture of propane and butane gas** is the most common variety. LPG is easy to store without losing energy and is also sold in bottles. It can be used for heating and cooking or for drying animal fodder; it can fuel vehicles, and may also be a propellant in a deodorant spray.

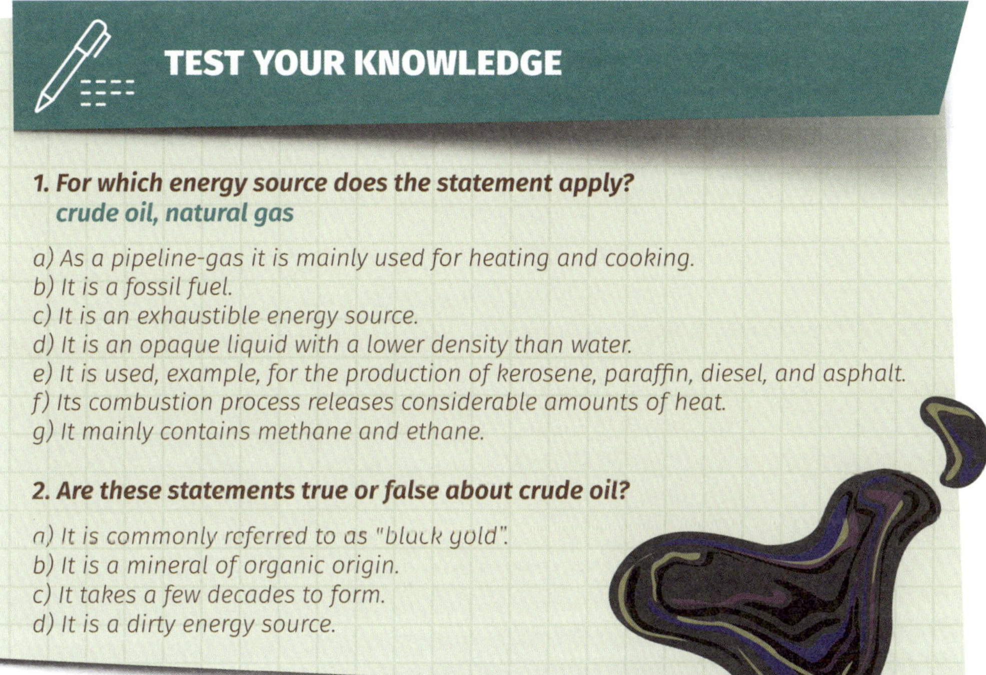

TEST YOUR KNOWLEDGE

1. *For which energy source does the statement apply?*
crude oil, natural gas

a) As a pipeline-gas it is mainly used for heating and cooking.
b) It is a fossil fuel.
c) It is an exhaustible energy source.
d) It is an opaque liquid with a lower density than water.
e) It is used, example, for the production of kerosene, paraffin, diesel, and asphalt.
f) Its combustion process releases considerable amounts of heat.
g) It mainly contains methane and ethane.

2. *Are these statements true or false about crude oil?*

a) It is commonly referred to as "black gold".
b) It is a mineral of organic origin.
c) It takes a few decades to form.
d) It is a dirty energy source.

30

LIFE UNDER OUR FEET

Soil is the uppermost, fertile layer of the Earth's crust. It is one of the foundations of life; it provides nutrients and water for plants and thus indirectly also for animals and humans.

WHAT IS SOIL MADE UP OF?

Soil is a complex, **three-phase system**. Its solid phase materials are the soil skeleton and the organic matter: i.e. decomposition products of dead organisms and excretion products of living organisms. The liquid phase is the ground moisture. Soil air fills the gaps between the soil grains.

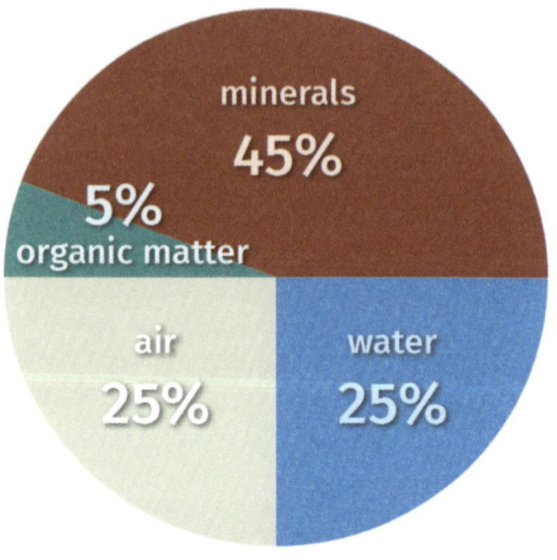

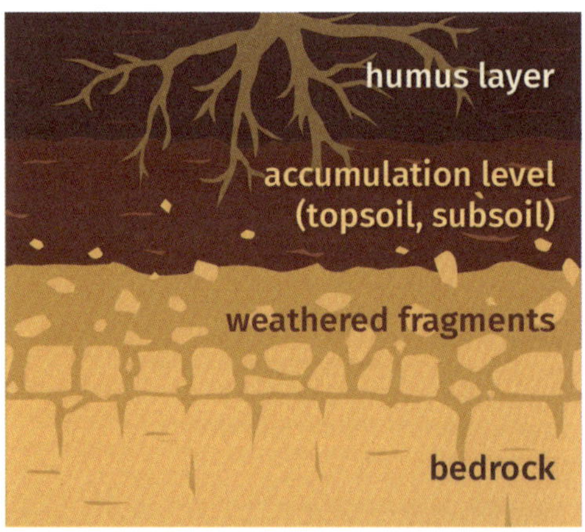

HUMUS

Humus is the most important component of soil. Plants absorb essential nutrients like nitrogen and phosphorus from humus. The darker the colour of the soil, the more humus it contains, and the more fertile it is.

SOIL FORMATION

Soil forms on bedrock. It is the parent material of soil formation. During weathering, external forces such as frost, wind, and water break up the larger rock fragments. Over time, microorganisms and other tiny creatures colonise the resulting regolith. As they die, **organic material** accumulates. This is how the fertile soil is created.

TEST YOUR KNOWLEDGE

1. Complete the text.

liquid, three-phase, excretion products, organic

Soil is a complex, ... system. Its solid phase materials are the soil skeleton and ..... matter: decomposition products of dead organisms and ..... of living organisms. ..... is present in ground moisture. Soil air fills the gaps between the soil grains.

2. What are the five steps of the soil formation process?

a) Organic material accumulates when living organisms die.
b) This creates fertile soil.
c) Regolith forms.
d) In the bedrock, external forces cause the larger rock fragments to break up.
e) Over time, microorganisms and other small organisms colonise the regolith.

☐ ☐ ☐ ☐ ☐

3. Mark the soil layers.

a) Weathered rock fragments
b) Bedrock
c) Accumulation level (topsoil, subsoil)
d) Humus layer

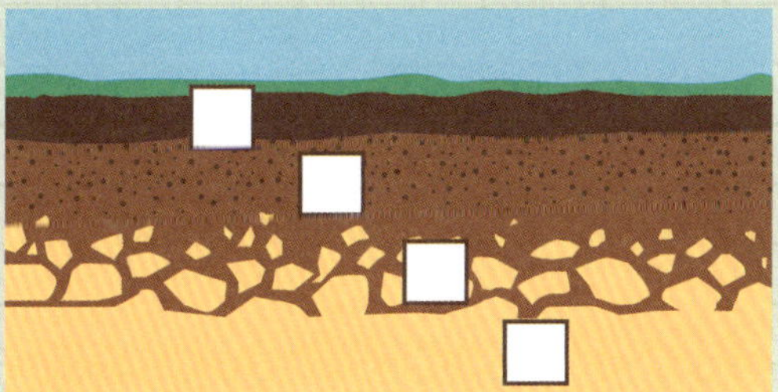

31

THE SEVENTH ELEMENT

Nitrogen makes up four fifths of the air. Along with carbon, hydrogen and oxygen, nitrogen is one of the four elements that are particularly important for the structure of living organisms.

WHAT DO WE KNOW?

Nitrogen is the 7th element in the periodic table, and it belongs to Group V. It occurs in nature in elemental form and in compounds. It was discovered by **Daniel Rutherford**.

PRIMARY BIOGENIC ELEMENT

The cells of living organisms consist in 99% of only four elements: carbon, hydrogen, oxygen, and nitrogen. These four are the primary biogenic elements. Many biologically important macromolecules, such as proteins, contain nitrogen atoms as building blocks.

CHEMISTRY OF NITROGEN

The nitrogen atom has the highest **electronegativity** after fluorine and oxygen. Elemental nitrogen is a linear, diatomic, non-polar molecule. There is a triple covalent bond between the nitrogen atoms, and each has one non-bonding electron pair. High energy is required to break the bonds of a nitrogen molecule. The nitrogen molecule is a very **stable**, non-polar molecule. At standard temperatures it reacts with practically nothing, therefore it is called an **inert gas**.

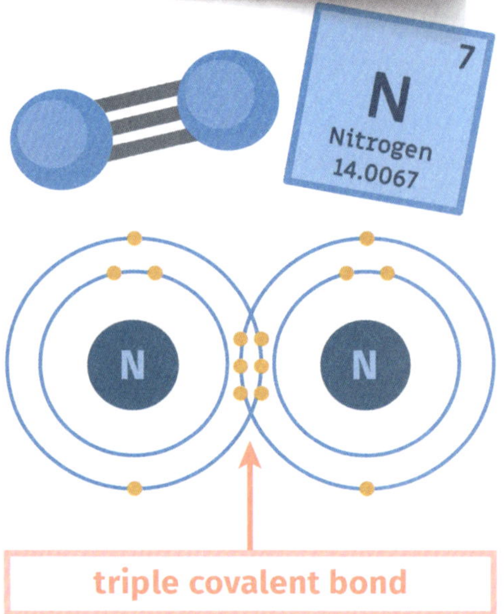

TEST YOUR KNOWLEDGE

1. True or false?

a) Nitrogen gas makes up about half of the air.
b) Nitrogen compounds are also found in minerals.
c) Nitrogen is a biogenic element, an important building block of living organisms.
d) Nitrogen was discovered by Marie Curie.
e) The nitrogen molecule is highly reactive and interacts readily.
f) Nitrogen is a Group V element.

2. Tick the box of items in which nitrogen gas is used.

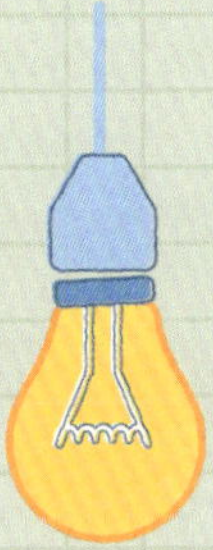

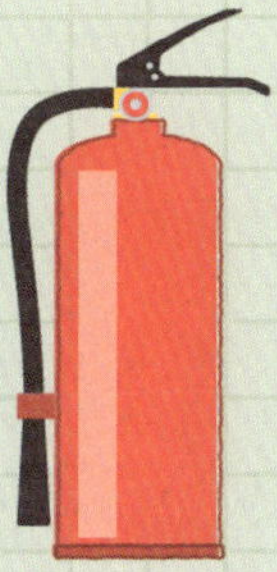

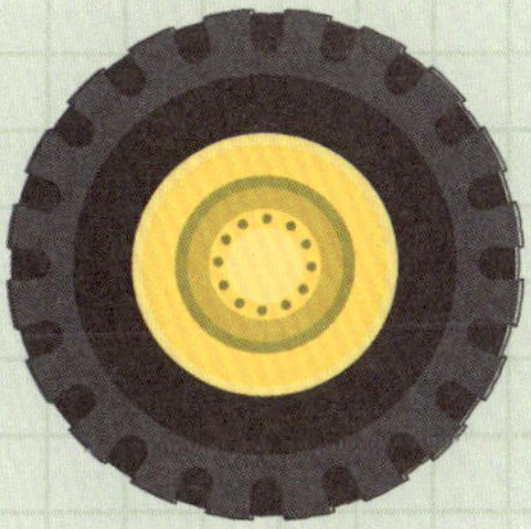

☐ ☐ ☐ ☐

32 WHERE ARE YOU, NITROGEN?

Elemental nitrogen is converted by nitrogen-fixing bacteria living in soil and water into nitrate ions, which are readily available to plants.

IN THE AIR, IN THE SOIL

Nitrogen makes up about 78 per cent of the air, but most living things cannot use nitrogen in its **elemental form**. Nitrogen-fixing bacteria take up nitrogen from the soil and convert it into ammonia. This is then oxidised by the soil's nitrifying bacteria to form nitrite and then nitrate ions, which are easily utilised by the roots due to their good solubility in water.

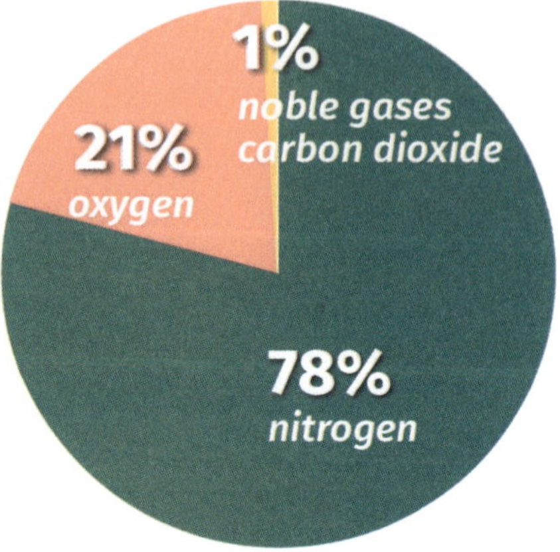

INSIDE THE PLANTS

In plants, nitrite and nitrate are reduced to **ammonium ions**, from which **organic** nitrogen compounds, such as amino acids, proteins, nucleic acids and chlorophyll pigments are made. Plants are an important source of nitrogen for heterotrophic organisms. When organisms die, once again, ammonia forms from their organic nitrogen compounds.

DID YOU KNOW?

Atmospheric nitrogen may be oxidised by lightning to nitrogen dioxide. This reacts with water to form nitric acid in precipitation.

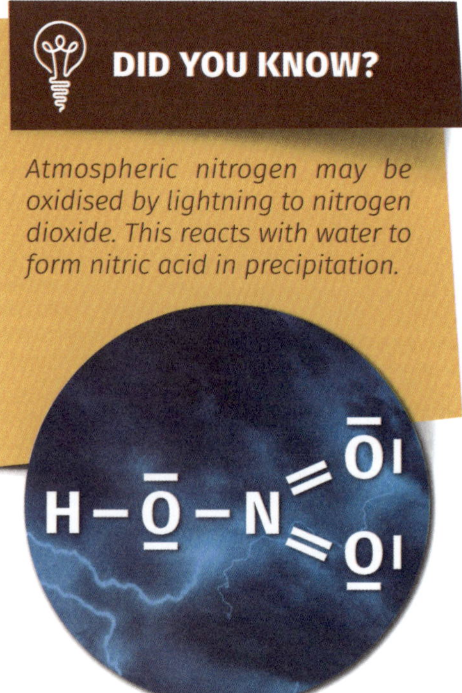

IS USING FERTILISERS HARMFUL?

Excessive use of nitrogen fertilisers can be harmful, as the accumulation of nitrite and nitrate ions in surface waters can cause **algal bloom** and **eutrophication**.

TEST YOUR KNOWLEDGE

1. Match the terms with the phenomenon.

a) These organisms live in root systems, and convert nitrogen to ammonia.
b) Most of it is not usable for living organisms.
c) It is composed of about 78 % nitrogen.
d) It can be harmful if used in excess.

1. Nitrogen fertiliser
2. Nitrogen-fixing bacteria
3. Air
4. Elemental nitrogen

2. Complete the text.

plants, nitrate, die, ammonium ions, ammonia

In ..... , nitrite and ..... are reduced to ..... , from which organic nitrogen compounds, amino acids, proteins, nucleic acids, and chlorophyll pigments are made. Plants are an important source of nitrogen for heterotrophic organisms. When organisms ..... , ... is formed again from their organic nitrogen compounds.

33 STATES OF MATTER

Substances can exist in different states of matter depending on their state variables.

GASES

Gas molecules move in a straight line until they collide with another gas molecule. Their thermal motion causes them to fill the available space, which causes the phenomenon called **diffusion**. The gas molecules are so far apart that ideally there is no interaction between them. According to **Avogadro's law**, any equal volume of gas under the same pressure and temperature conditions contains the same number of particles.

LIQUIDS

There is considerable cohesion between liquid molecules that holds the particles together. Liquids have a fixed **volume**, are incompressible (or can only be compressed by extreme pressure) and take the shape of the container. Particles move in a rolling motion, continuously replacing each other.

SOLIDS

In solids, the **cohesion** between molecules is **so strong** that not only is their volume constant, but also their shape. Solids can be amorphous or crystalline.

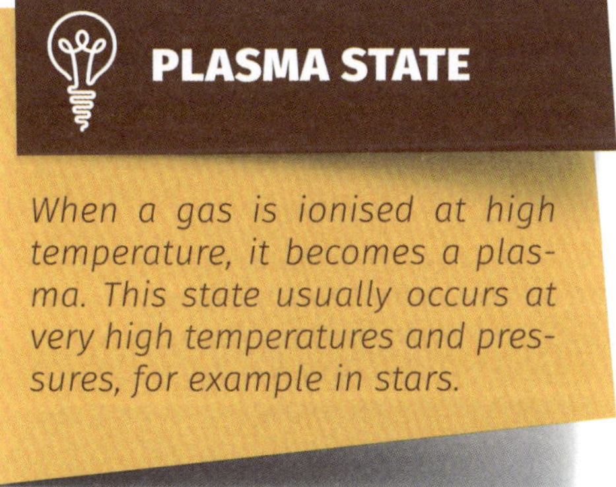

PLASMA STATE

When a gas is ionised at high temperature, it becomes a plasma. This state usually occurs at very high temperatures and pressures, for example in stars.

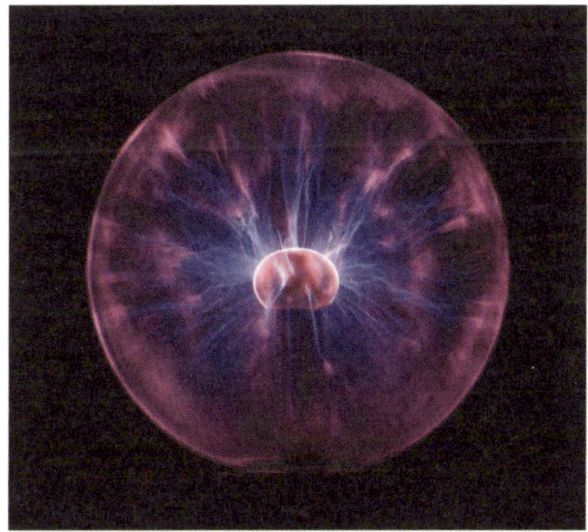

TEST YOUR KNOWLEDGE

1. Match the state of matter to the description.
gas, liquid, solid

a) Its molecules move in a straight line until they collide with another molecule.
b) They have a defined volume, they take the shape of the container.
c) They can have amorphous or crystalline structure.
d) Individual particles move in a rolling motion.
e) Their volume and shape are constant due to the strong interaction between the particles.

34

POTATOES A'LA DARWIN

The change of state of certain substances, such as freezing, melting, vaporization, boiling and condensing, is a familiar process from everyday experience.

PHASE TRANSITIONS

Freezing, melting, vaporization, boiling and condensation are **first-order** phase transitions. During the transitions, the physical properties of the material undergo a sudden change. The temperature points at which the change happens (e.g. melting and freezing points) are characteristic of the material, but also depend on other factors, mainly pressure. The melting point of solids generally increases with pressure.

INTERESTING

The boiling point of water decreases with pressure. ***Charles Darwin*** *observed this on his journey through the Andes. "At the place where we slept water necessarily boiled, from the diminished pressure of the atmosphere, at a lower temperature than it does in a less lofty country (...) Hence the potatoes, after remaining for some hours in the boiling water, were nearly as hard as ever." (Naturalist's Voyage Round the World)*

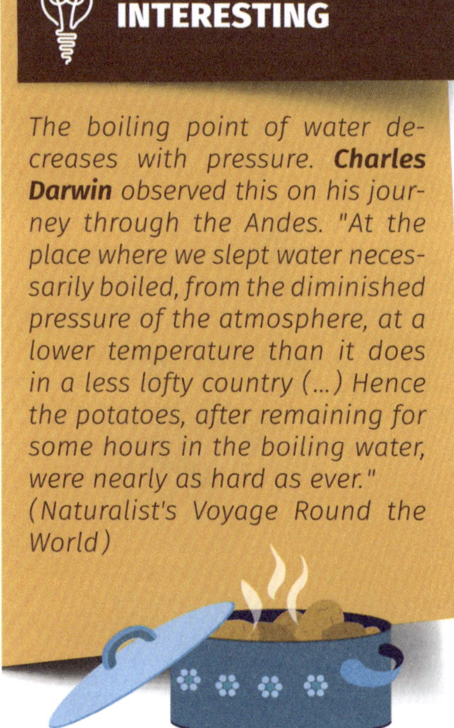

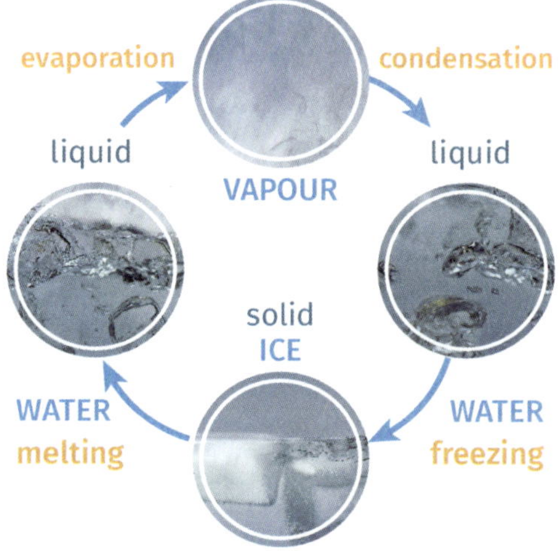

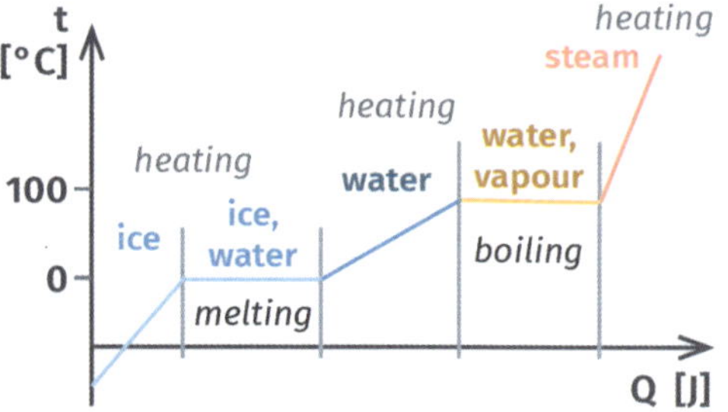

DYNAMIC EQUILIBRIUM

Above a liquid that evaporates or boils in a **closed space**, the saturated vapour of the liquid is in dynamic equilibrium with the liquid, i.e. the **number of molecules** leaving and returning to the liquid is **equal** in a given unit of time. The state in which, on average, the same number of transformations take place in both directions in a reversible process is called dynamic equilibrium.

TEST YOUR KNOWLEDGE

1. True or false?

a) Darwin found that water boiled more slowly at higher altitudes, making it more difficult to cook potatoes.
b) The melting point and the freezing point are examples of temperature points.
c) The melting point of solids generally increases with pressure.
d) The boiling point of water decreases with pressure.

35

SEAWATER AS A SOLUTION

A solution is defined as a multi-component liquid system in which the amount of one component is much greater than the amount of the others. In daily life, we most often encounter aqueous solutions.

SOLUTION

A solution is a **homogeneous** multi-component system, where no surface boundaries can be observed between the components, even with a microscope. The **solvent** is usually a liquid, and the other component can be a solid, liquid or gas. This is called the **solute**. Typically, the amount of solvent is much greater than that of the solute.

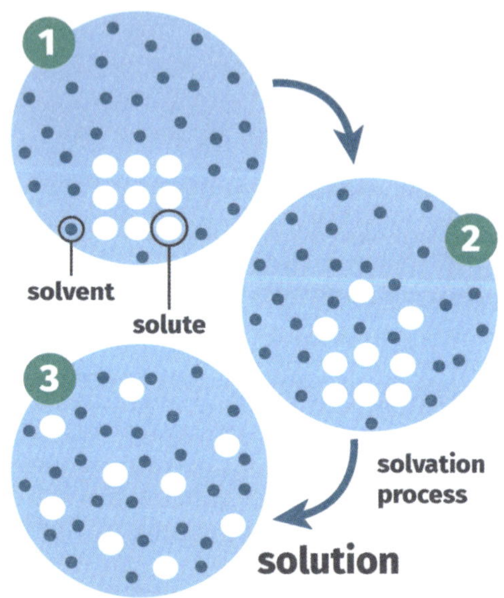

SEAS AND OCEANS

The salt content of sea- and ocean water is significantly higher than that of freshwater. The average salinity is 3.5%, which means that one litre of seawater contains 35 grams of salt. **The salt content of different seas varies.** For example, the salinity of the Baltic Sea is 1%, much lower than the average, while that of the Mediterranean Sea is higher than average at 4%. The highest salt content is found in the inland seas, with the Dead Sea having a salt content of 28-30%.

HOW IS SALT EXTRACTED FROM THE SEA?

The seawater is fed into large, shallow tanks from which the **water evaporates**. This process is repeated several times while the solution is undergoes various types of treatment. The thick, clear, salty juice is then transferred to another tank and crystallised. The salt is ground in mills to the desired grain size. Sea salt contains natural iodine in quantities of up to 5 mg/kg.

TEST YOUR KNOWLEDGE

1. True or false?

a) Solutions are liquid multi-component systems, in which one component is much more abundant than the others.
b) In everyday life, we most often encounter oily solutions.
c) Solutions are homogeneous system.
d) Both components in a solution are liquid.
e) In a solution, one component is the solvent, and the other component is the solute.
f) Solutions are characterised by the quantity of the dissolved substance, whereby the amount of solute is much greater than that of the solvent.

2. Complete the text.
4%, 35 g, 28-30%, 3,5%, 1%

The average salt content of sea- and ocean water is ..... , which means that each litre if seawater contains ..... of salt in solution.. The salt content of different seas varies. For example, the Baltic Sea contains ..... salt, while the Mediterranean Sea ..... . The highest salt content is found in the inland seas, with the Dead Sea having a salt content of ..... .

36 SOLVENTS

Solutions consist of solvents and dissolved substances. But how much of one substance can be dissolved in another substance?

WHAT DISSOLVES IN WHAT?

Different substances can dissolve well, weakly, or not at all in a solvent. The rule of thumb is that **"like dissolves like"**. Non-polar solvents (e.g. white/surgical spirit that can be used to clean the area around minor wounds or to cleanse makeup brushes), tend to dissolve non-polar substances, while polar solvents (e.g. water) tend to dissolve polar molecules and ionic crystals. Certain substances, such as **acetone**, contain both polar and non-polar parts, and are therefore good solvents of both polar and non-polar materials. Acetone unrestrictedly mixes with both polar water and non-polar chloroform and dissolves most plastics well.

SOLVENT	
POLAR	NON-POLAR
• water • alcohol • ethanol	• petrol • chloroform • carbon tetrachloride

SATURATED & UNSATURATED

An unsaturated solution can still dissolve more of the solute at the **given temperature**. If the solution cannot dissolve any more of solute at the given temperature it is saturated. Solute added in excess **remains solid**.

SOLUBILITY

Solubility is usually expressed as the number of grams of solute that can be dissolved in 100 grams of a solvent at a given temperature.

SUPERSATURATED SOLUTIONS

When a solution that has been saturated at a high temperature is cooled, it may become supersaturated. Because supersaturated solutions **contain more solute** than what is normally possible, they are unstable, and **may rapidly crystallize**.

BEAUTIFUL PRECIPITATE

Karstification is also related to the dissolution process: well-soluble, solid bedrock slowly dissolves in water. As carbon dioxide escapes from the solution, calcium carbonate starts to precipitate, creating stalactites and stalagmites in caves.

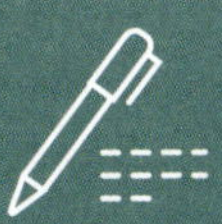

TEST YOUR KNOWLEDGE

1. Match the terms with the descriptions.
crystals, acetone, water, karstification, solubility

a) Rock with a readily soluble, solid structure is dissolved by water.
b) They precipitate in a supersaturated solution.
c) The number of grams of a substance that can be dissolved in 100 grams of a solvent at a given temperature.
d) The most common, everyday polar solvent.
e) It unrestrictedly mixes with polar water and non-polar chloroform..

37

THE MESSAGE OF THE CABBAGE

Acidic? Alkaline? Neutral? The pH scale created by Soren Peter Lauritz Sorensen, a Danish biochemist, is used to describe solutions – including aqueous ones. The pH value ranges from 0 to 14.

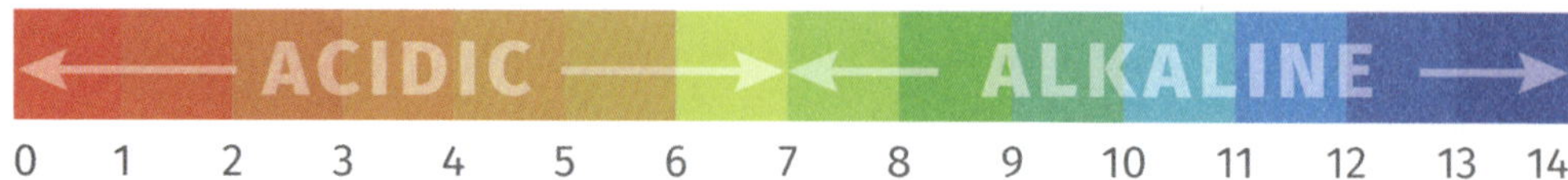

pH VALUE

The pH value can be represented using a scale from 0 to 14. An aqueous solution is called **neutral** when the measured pH is 7. A lower pH value indicates an **acidic** solution, a higher pH value an **alkaline** solution. Tap water has a pH value of 7, so it is neutral.

CHEMISTRY BEHIND THE pH

Some compounds tend to trade their **hydrogen ions** when dissolved in water. Substances that donate their hydrogen ions are called **acids**, while the ones that pick these ions up are **bases**. The aqueous solution of bases is alkaline (pH >7), that of acids is acidic (pH<7).

INDICATORS

Indicators are substances that show the pH of a solution by **changing colour**. Different indicators can be used for measurements, such as phenolphthalein, litmus, or methyl orange. These indicators produce variable colour changes in different media.

TESTS

What do we see when we add lemon juice, tap water, or soap solution into **phenolphthalein**? There is no change in the first two, but it turns purple on contact with the alkali. If we use **litmus** instead of phenolphtalein it turns magenta in lemon juice, purple in tap water and blue in soapy water. **Methyl orange** is red-orange in an acid, and in neutral tap water and soapy water it turns yelow.

Phenolphthalein		Litmus		Methyl orange	
acidic		acidic		acidic	
neutral		neutral		neutral	
alkaline		alkaline		alkaline	

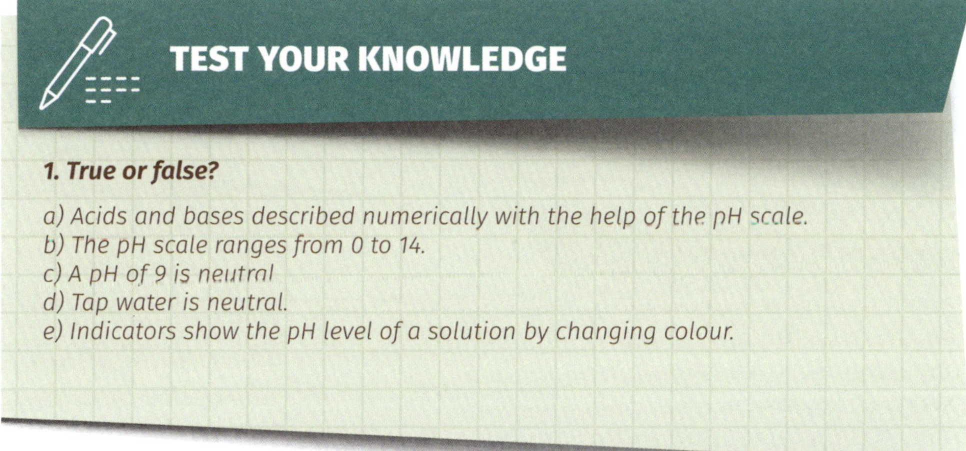

TEST YOUR KNOWLEDGE

1. True or false?

a) Acids and bases described numerically with the help of the pH scale.
b) The pH scale ranges from 0 to 14.
c) A pH of 9 is neutral
d) Tap water is neutral.
e) Indicators show the pH level of a solution by changing colour.

38

GASES

The best-known gas mixture on Earth is air, which consists of 78 % nitrogen and 21 % oxygen; containing less than 1 % noble gases and 0.04 % carbon dioxide.

OXYGEN

Oxygen is the third most abundant chemical element in the universe after hydrogen and helium but **the most abundant in the Earth's biosphere**. In nature, it is in a constant cycle. Certain organisms and all industries consume large amounts of oxygen. The oxygen content of the air is replenished by the photosynthesis of green plants, hence the protection of the Earth's vegetation is of utmost importance.

TRACE GASES

Components that occur only in traces in the air are called trace gases. ***These include carbon dioxide, noble gases, methane or water vapour.***

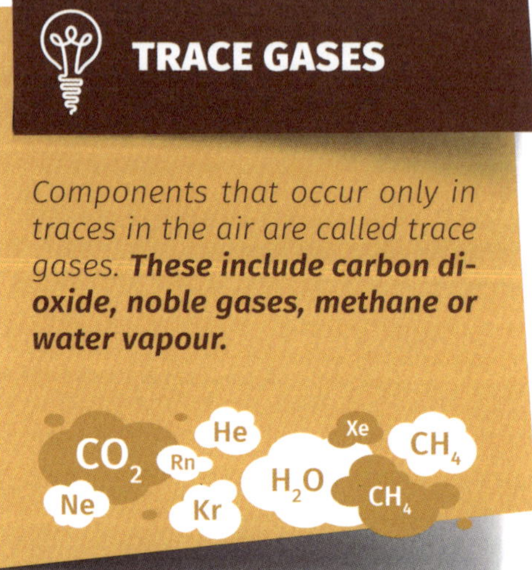

CARBON DIOXIDE

Carbon dioxide is a colourless, odourless, non-toxic gas. It is heavier than air and **can cause breathing problems** if it accumulates in the lower layers of a closed room and displaces oxygen. Because it is non-flammable, it is also used in fire extinguishers to fight fires. Carbon dioxide is highly soluble in water; its aqueous solution is carbonic acid (**H_2CO_3**). It is best known as a component of bubbly drinks.

HYDROGEN

Hydrogen is the smallest, simplest atom. It is **the third most common element on Earth** after oxygen and silicon. Hydrogen gas is colourless, odourless, and 14.5 times less dense than air; it is practically insoluble in water. In its elemental state, it occurs in small quantities in the upper layers of the Earth's atmosphere, in volcanic gases, and in the vapours of hot springs. In **compounds**, it is most abundant in water, which covers 71% of the Earth's surface.

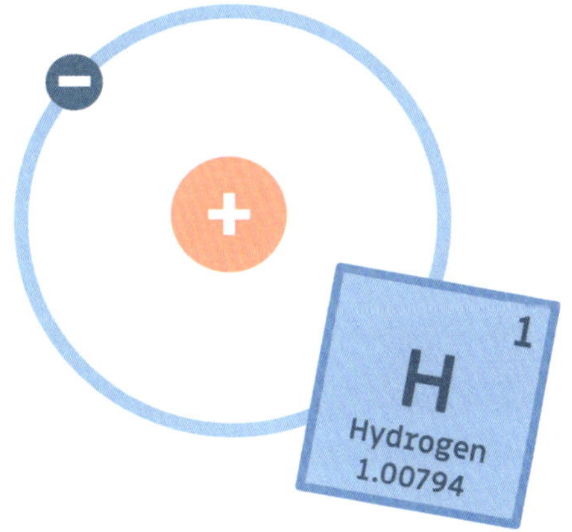

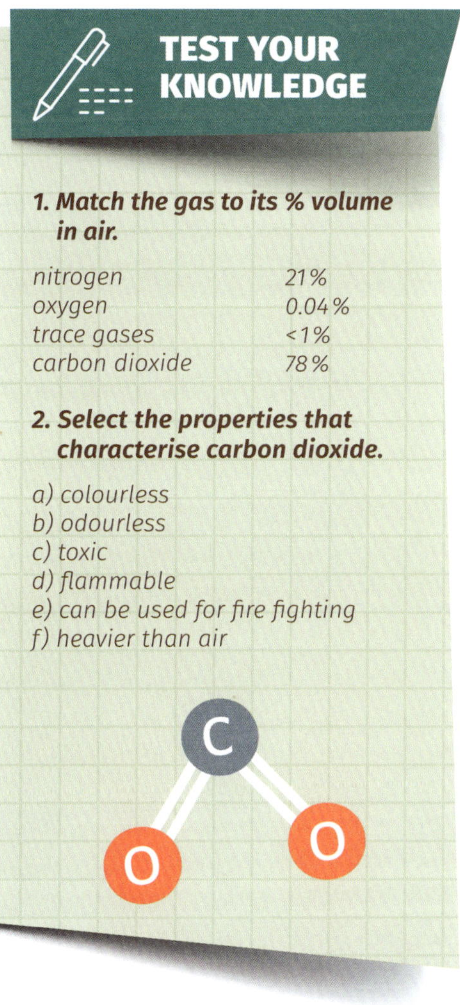

TEST YOUR KNOWLEDGE

1. Match the gas to its % volume in air.

nitrogen	*21%*
oxygen	*0.04%*
trace gases	*<1%*
carbon dioxide	*78%*

2. Select the properties that characterise carbon dioxide.

a) colourless
b) odourless
c) toxic
d) flammable
e) can be used for fire fighting
f) heavier than air

39

DIRTY BUSINESS

The biosphere is a living system. However, the gas balance in the atmosphere has been disturbed by human activities. Increasing greenhouse gases, global warming, ozone depletion, and acid rain pose a serious threat to our planet.

AIR POLLUTION

Transport, industrial and agricultural activities, burning of forests and increased use of fossil fuels release large amounts of carbon dioxide and other gases into the atmosphere. About 20% of the world's population breathes heavily polluted air. In addition, **greenhouse gases** trap heat from the Earth's surface and radiate it back. The greenhouse effect is a major contributor to climate change and sea level rise.

THINNING OF THE OZONE LAYER

The phenomenon of ozone depletion and the size of the ozone hole that forms each year have taken on dramatic proportions, especially over the regions with the lowest temperatures on Earth, the polar regions. The ozone layer over Antarctica has now been reduced by almost half. The thinning ozone layer **does not provide sufficient protection** against harmful ultraviolet rays.

ACID RAIN

Pollutants in the air react with other substances and form acids. Acid rain pollutes the environment and damages our health.

DIRTY TERMS

Emissions: *discharge of air pollutants*
Immission: *the concentration of pollutants in the air*

WHAT IS SMOG?

London smog is caused by the **burning of coal** in windless, cool and humid weather. Los Angeles smog is caused by **pollutants emitted by traffic** in sunny, windless weather.

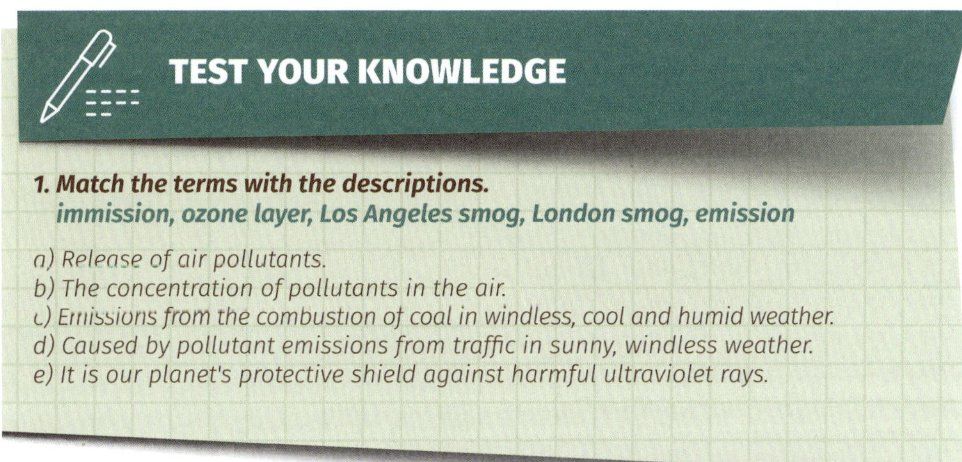

TEST YOUR KNOWLEDGE

1. *Match the terms with the descriptions.*
immission, ozone layer, Los Angeles smog, London smog, emission

a) Release of air pollutants.
b) The concentration of pollutants in the air.
c) Emissions from the combustion of coal in windless, cool and humid weather.
d) Caused by pollutant emissions from traffic in sunny, windless weather.
e) It is our planet's protective shield against harmful ultraviolet rays.

40

UNDER A PROTECTIVE SHIELD

The change in temperature is the simplest way to distinguish the layers of the atmosphere. Up to an altitude of almost 1000 km, four layers make up the atmosphere. Their boundaries are marked by a decrease or increase in temperature.

TROPOSPHERE

The layer closest to the Earth's surface is the **troposphere**, which is 10-12 km thick. This is where the weather phenomena take place. This layer contains almost all the water in the atmosphere. Temperatures in the upper regions are only -56 °C. Most aircraft fly at the upper boundary of the troposphere.

STRATOSPHERE

In the **stratosphere**, at altitudes between 10 and 50 km, temperatures gradually rise. In the upper regions, it reaches 10 °C. The temperature rise is due to the **ozone layer**, which absorbs most of the Sun's harmful ultraviolet light.

MESOSPHERE

In the **mesosphere** above the stratosphere, temperatures drop again. The coldest part (between -90 and -120 °C) is found near the top of this layer, at an altitude of 85 km.

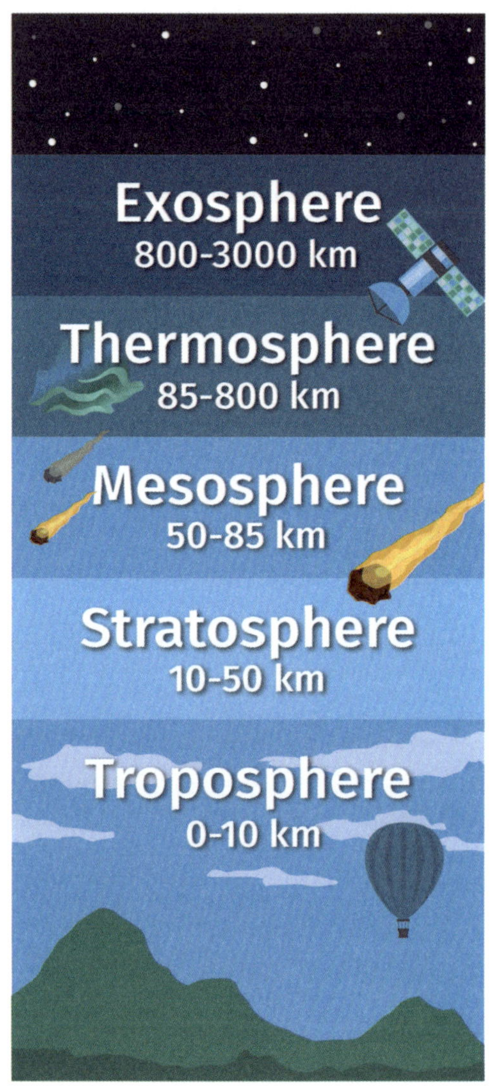

THERMOSPHERE

In the **thermosphere** above the mesosphere, the temperature rises similarly to the stratosphere (around 1000 °C) due to the absorption of ultraviolet radiation. This layer is also called the **ionosphere** because it consists of ions, which are good conductors of electricity.

TEST YOUR KNOWLEDGE

1. Which atmospheric layer is described?

This layer is also called the ionosphere because it consists of ions, which are good conductors of electricity.

....

2. Match the temperature with the atmospheric layer.

Troposphere	*10 °C*
Stratosphere	*−90 and −120 °C*
Mesosphere	*1000 °C*
Thermosphere	*−56 °C*

ANSWERS

1) OUR COSMIC HOME

1. True or false?

a) true; b) false; c) false; d) false; e) true

2) OUR ETERNAL COMPANION

1. Match the terms with the descriptions.

a) moon rocks; b) lunar eclipse; c) solar eclipse; d) Theia; e) total solar eclipse

2. True or false?

a) true; b) false; c) true

3) COLD & HOT

1. True or false?

a) true; b) true; c) false; d) true; e) false

4) BIRTH OF GIANTS

1. Match the process with the description.

collision of two oceanic rock plates: ***b)***
collision of two continental rock plates: ***a)***

2. Match the natural formations with the way they were formed.

When two oceanic rock plates collide. **the Japanese Islands, New Britain Archipelago**
Oceanic and continental rock plates collide. **the Andes, Cordillera**
When two continental rock slabs collide. **the Himalayas**

5) GIANTS ON FIRE

2. Match the terms with the definitions.

a) Stromboli; b) magma; c) lava; d) hot spot; e) pillow lava

6) IT'S MOVING THERE!

1. Match the terms with the definitions.

a) seismograph; b) Richter scale; c) hypocentre; d) magnitude; e) Mercalli scale

7) WONDERFUL STALACTITES

1. True or false?

a) true b) false c) true d) false

2. Match the terms with the definitions.

a) Devil's plough b) doline c) polje d) sinkhole

8) COLD, SLIGHTLY WARM, HOT!

1. True or false?

a) true; b) true; c) true; d) false

2. Match the solar zones with the descriptions.

The area between the Tropic of Cancer and the Tropic of Capricorn. **hot zone**
The area between the poles and the polar circles. **cold zone**
The area between the tropics and the polar circles. **temperate zone**

3. **Write the important latitudes on the globe.**

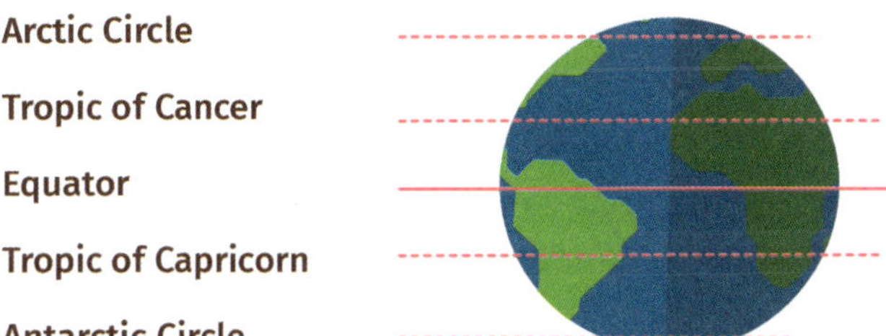

9) CLIMBING THROUGH CLIMATES

1. **Complete the text.**

Temperatures in the mountain areas are year-round **lower**, and the annual precipitation is **high** than in the surrounding climatic zone. With increasing altitude, the corresponding climatic **zones** are formed. The levelling is represented by the climate-adjusted **vegetation**.

2. **Write the names of the boundaries separating the zones.**

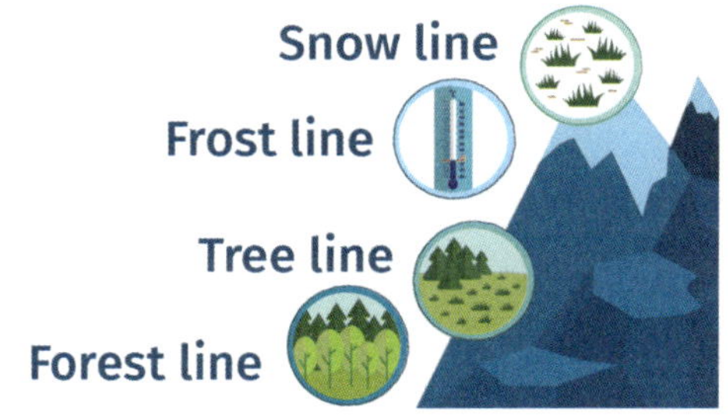

10) WIND IN THE SKY

1. **Match the terms with the definitions.**

a) Coriolis force; b) monsoon; c) polar winds; d) westerly winds

2. **True or false?**

a) true; b) true; c) false; d) false; e) true

11) WEATHER FRONTS

1. **Match the terms with the definitions.**

a) cyclones; b) fronts; c) wind; d) anticyclone; e) air pressure

2. **True or false?**

a) true; b) true; c) true; d) true

12) MOISTURE IN THE AIR

1. **Match the terms with the definitions.**

a) dew; b) dew point; c) absolute humidity, d) condensation nuclei

13) THE SOURCE OF LIFE

1. **True or false?**

a) true; b) true; c) false; d) true; e) false; f) true

14) WATER, WATER, EVERYWHERE

1. Match the terms with the descriptions.

a) hydrosphere; b) solar radiation; c) evaporation; d) seas; e) World Ocean

2. Put the process of water supply cycles in ascending order based on their duration.

1. the water supply of the atmosphere
2. the water supply of the rivers
3. the water resources of the oceans

15) THE WATER CYCLE

1. Complete the text.

The majority of water molecules in surface waters **evaporate** into the atmosphere as a result of heat causing the hydrogen bonds to break and form water **vapour**. When water vapour settles due to pressure and temperature changes, **clouds** are formed. Precipitation also carries **polluting** substances from the air.

16) SURFACE WATERS

1. Match the terms with the definitions.

a) watercourse; b) water yield; c) water flow regime; d) flood; e) water level

17) UNDER THE SURFACE...

1. Match the terms with the descriptions.

a) soil moisture; b) artesian water; c) thermal water; d) mineral water

18) ATOMIC MODELS

1. Match the names with the facts.

a) Dalton; b) Thomson; c) Becquerel

19) INSIDE THE ATOM

1. Match the terms with the descriptions.

a) nucleus; b) oxygen; c) valence shell; d) first shell

2. True or false?

a) true; b) true; c) false; d) true; e) false; f) true

20) THE WORLD'S COMPOSITION

1. Match the name of the element with its origin.

a) hydrogen; b) phosphorus; c) oxygen; d) mercury; e) bromine

2. Assign the name of the element to the scientist it was named after.

a) Einsteinium; b) Mendelevium; c) Fermium; d) Nobelium; e) Curium

21) WHY IS IT THE WAY IT IS?

1. Match the lattice structures to the pictures.

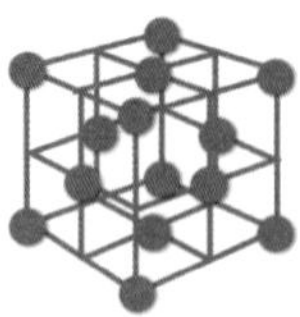

Face-centred cubic (fcc) crystal lattice

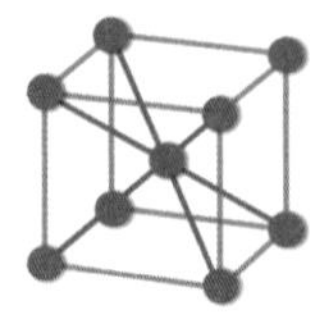

body-centred cubic (bcc) crystal lattice

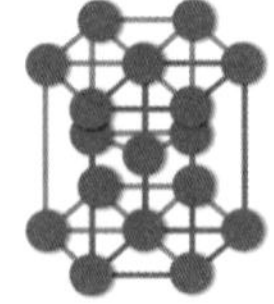

hexagonal close packed (hcp) crystal lattice

22) BLACK DIAMONDS

1. Tick the correct statements.

a); b); c); e); f); h)

2. Write the matching names next to the pictures.

23) TRIPLETS

1. For which allotrope of carbon is the statement true?

a) graphite; b) diamond; c) diamond; d) graphite; e) diamond

24) SECRET OF THE MINES

1. Complete the text.

In the hydrothermal **ore precipitation** process, ground water leaches metals from **magmatic** rock. The ore deposits of precious metals and **non-ferrous metals** (zinc, lead, copper) are formed by hydrothermal ore precipitation.

2. Tick the statements that apply to metals.

a); b); d)

25) SEDIMENTARY ROCKS

1. Match the sedimentary rock types to the descriptions.

a) debris; b) chemical; c) organic

2. Mark the statements that do not apply to aluminium.

c)

26) STRIKE WHILE IT IS HOT

1. Tick the statements that apply to iron.

a); b); d); e)

2. Match the iron compound to the description.

a) iron sulphide; b) Pyrite; c) ferrous sulphate

3. True or false?

a) true; b) true; c) true; d) false; e) true; f) true; g) true

27) THE QUEEN OF METALS

1. True or false?

a) false; b) true; c) false; d) true; e) true; f) false

28) GOLDEN SHINE

1. True or false?

a) true; b) false; c) false; d) true; e) true; f) false

2. Choose the correct solution. What can gold be dissolved in?

- [ ] *Hydrochloric acid*
- [x] *Aqua regia*
- [ ] *Nitric acid*

29) EXHAUSTIBLE ENERGY RESOURCES

1. For which energy source does the statement apply?

crude oil: d), e); ***natural gas:*** a), g); ***crude oil + natural gas:*** b), c), f)

2. Are these statements true or false about crude oil?

a) true; b) true; c) false; d) true

30) LIFE UNDER OUR FEET

1. Complete the text.

Soil is a complex, **three-phase** system. Its solid phase materials are the soil skeleton and **organic** matter: decomposition products of dead organisms and **excretion products** of living organisms. **Liquid** is present in ground moisture. Soil air fills the gaps between the soil grains.

2. What are the five steps of the soil formation process?

1 d); 2 c); 3 e); 4 a); 5 b)

3. Mark the soil layers.

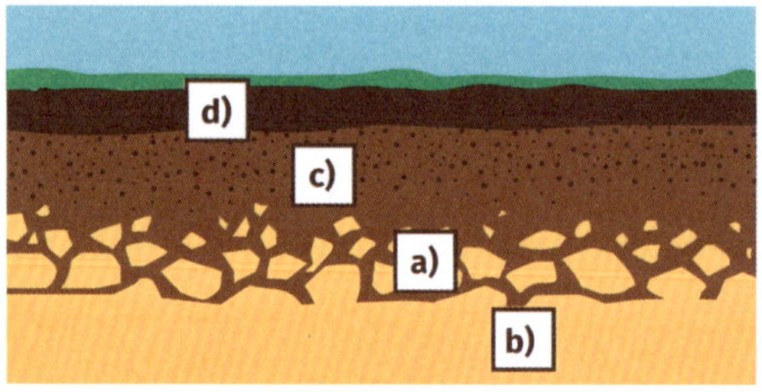

31) THE SEVENTH ELEMENT

1. True or false?

a) false; b) true; c) true; d) false; e) false; f) true

2. Tick the box of items in which nitrogen gas is used.

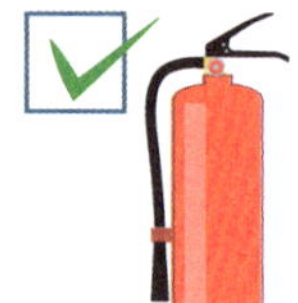

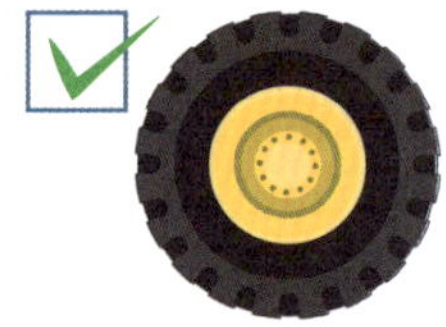

32) WHERE ARE YOU, NITROGEN?

1. Match the terms with the phenomenon.

a) 2; b) 4; c) 3; d) 1

2. Complete the text.

In **plants,** nitrite and **nitrate** are reduced to **ammonium ions**, from which organic nitrogen compounds, amino acids, proteins, nucleic acids, and chlorophyll pigments are made. Plants are an important source of nitrogen for heterotrophic organisms. When organisms **die**, **ammonia** is formed again from their organic nitrogen compounds.

33) STATES OF MATTER

1. Match the state of matter to the description.

a) gas; b) liquid; c) solid; d) liquid; e) solid

34) POTATOES A'LA DARWIN

1. True or false?

a) true; b) true; c) true; d) true

35) SEAWATER AS A SOLUTION

1. True or false?

a) true; b) false; c) true; d) false; e) true; f) false

2. Complete the text.

The average salt content of sea- and ocean water is **3,5%**, which means that each litre if sea-water contains **35 g** of salt in solution. The salt content of water from different seas varies. For example, the Baltic Sea contains **1%** salt, the Mediterranean Sea **4%**. The highest salt content is found in the inland seas, with the Dead Sea having a salt content of **28-30%**.

36) SOLVENTS

1. Match the terms with the descriptions.

a) karstification; b) crystals; c) solubility; d) water; e) acetone

37) THE MESSAGE OF THE CABBAGE

1. True or false?

a) true; b) true; c) false; d) true; e) true

38) GASES

1. Match the gas to its % volume in air.

nitrogen: 78%; oxygen: 21%; trace gases: <1%; carbon dioxide: 0,04%

2. Select the properties that characterise carbon dioxide.

a); b); e); f)

39) DIRTY BUSINESS

1. Match the terms with the descriptions.

a) emission; b) immission; c) London smog; d) Los Angeles smog; e) ozon layer

40) UNDER A PROTECTIVE SHIELD

1. Which atmoshperic layer is described?

Thermosphere

2. Match the temperature with the atmospheric layer.

Troposphere −56 °C
Stratosphere 10 °C
Mezosphere −90 and −120 °C
Thermosphere 1000 °C

TABLE OF CONTENTS

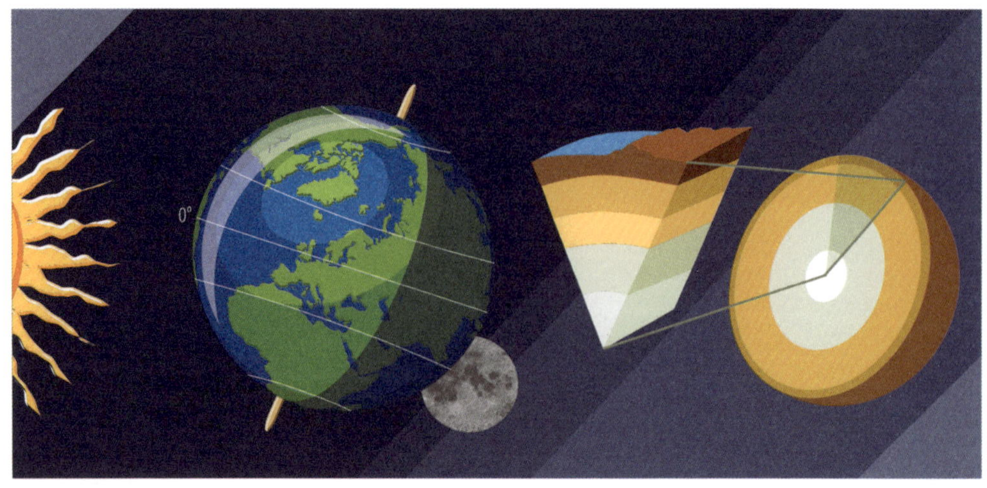